BOB STEWAl

The Waters of The Gap

The Mythology of Aquae Sulis

Contents

The Goddess

The Gorgon's Head

How to use this Book

The study of mythology is complex and subtle, and involves constant reference to a group of basic patterns, structures, symbols and demonstrative stories.

To recreate the mythical and religious pattern of a specific site is a matter of combining intuition with hard research and detective work; and while this process is extremely difficult for many places, the comparative wealth of evidence available for Aquae Sulis makes the number of cross-references and essential items considerable.

The present analysis deals with the major symbols, and with the nature of the physical site itself, and the supportive symbols of related gods and goddesses and certain inscriptions are given a secondary place; particularly as these factors will be improved upon by further archaeological research, whereas the constant primary elements are the permanent framework within which the supportive factors evolved.

The book, therefore, may be used in a twofold manner. It may be read as a coherent argument and study of pagan symbolism in general, and in particular as it relates to the site of Aquae Sulis with its specific examples of general practices. It may also be used as a rapid reference source, as a detailed page by page list of contents has been supplied, which may even be used while visiting the museum and the site. With this end in mind, the separate sections have overlapping conents in many cases, and the general argument and analysis is followed by specific sections of supportive evidence. (For example, the linguistic elements of the discussion are touched upon briefly in several places where they may be necessary for rapid reference, while a more detailed exposition of their possible relevance is given separately. This same approach is used for the medieval chronicle material, and for the myth of King Bladud).

Finally, the book is intended for the general reader who has an interest in ancient matters, and who is prepared to forge ahead and make further study for themselves. Much of the finer detailed evidence is already available in major works in publication, and the purpose of this book is to bridge the gaps that exist between many of these works, and then refer the evidence directly to Aquae Sulis itself. There is no need for the reader to reach for major reference works while dealing with this book, and it is not set out in the traditional scholarly manner that bristles with footnotes and cross references. On the other hand, the few references given and recommended will provide more than sufficient cross reference material for those that seek to check in the traditional manner, and will also open out a new world of interest to those who are not familiar with some or any of the various fields of study that have contributed to the present work.

In the same way that the Baths and Temple of Aquae Sulis were smaller and specific examples of the great religious and magical edifices of the ancient world, so is this analysis of their symbolism, and religious use a compact and defined attempt to synthesize elements of major disciplines that deal with ancient matters in general.

An Introduction
To
British Mythology

British mythology is a vast and complicated subject, as indeed is *all* mythology. How often have we heard the phrase...."well, it's only a *myth*, after all...." or something similar? Many people, often quite intelligent people, think that myths are nothing more nor less than the idle fantasies of simple minds, the amusement of our ignorant ancestors who were not enlightened by technology or television. The word 'myth' is frequently used to mean 'that which is untrue', but a myth is by no means identical with a lie, and only *very* carefully constructed lies can emerge in time as myths by fitting into an existing mythical framework.

What, then, is a *myth*, what is this 'mythical framework'? Firstly, it must be admitted, frankly confessed, that myths *do* contain a large proportion of illogical material in their content, and that they should never be considered as literal truth. A brief look at any orthodox religion will show how difficult it is to take myths and wrench them into factual reality or history by use of authority or legality.

More important is the fact that myths in general do not represent superficial ignorance, or lack of perception on the part of their originators. Myths were not, as has often been suggested, mere rationalisations of phenomena in nature, for they were symbolic of *known* processes that occur in the interrelationship of humankind and the environment. Ancient symbology was not an attempt at explanation, but a suggestion of *pattern*, of *integration*, whereby categorisation or analysis was less important than mutual interaction between humans, the natural world, and the mysterious powers that originated all life and events. The processes shown in myths still hold good today, though the action is often transferred to slightly less obvious levels. The reaction with hostile powers of nature, for example, may have become the struggle to exist within an economic system....but the ways to balance and realisation shown in the old stories about gods, goddesses and heroes, still apply to the human psyche.

Three main branches are derived from the roots of pagan mythology and its related practices. The first is formal religion, with its various special organisations, sects and offshoots. The second is mental therapy, which is a modern re-statement of the human inner processes and patterns once symbolised by myth and magic. This second branch uses the same material as the first, but with marginally different methods, and a formidable technical jargon, neatly sidestepping the existence or non-existence of 'god'. The third branch is folklore, including at its most complex levels modern occultism, and mysticism derived from pagan and Christian unorthodox or 'heretical' sources. Folklore is an amorphous mass of loosely related symbols, in the form of tales, plays, images, song, music and ritual drama.

This third branch has inherited most from the pagan past, for it has been maintained by a strong oral tradition, where material is handed down through the centuries with remarkable continuity, and is refreshed by a constant regeneration of the basic mythical themes on a spontaneous or unconscious level; the same level wherein such myths first developed. Folklore is by no means a lost subject, or something that disappeared with the destruction of widespread rural communities. It exists in many different forms, right in the heart of the big city, and still lives in many country districts isolated enough to have traditions traceable to the medieval period or earlier. Furthermore, folklore grows and transmutes often dull subjects into living symbols which may be recognised as myths.

Perhaps the simplest way to illustrate this continuing process, without overcomplicated arguments and references is by example, by telling a thoroughly modern folktale. We can then see how this tale is actually part of 'British mythology', as it came from English people in modern London, but can be traced back to typical pagan imagery and belief from the pre-Christian era.

A few years ago, in the late 1960's and early 1970's, a very popular musician called Jimi Hendrix captured the imagination of millions of people. He set new standards of proficiency and style for electric guitar that radically changed the music industry. He followed a remarkably successful career; then committed suicide.

Not long after Hendrix's death, I was recording music in a London studio, and the technicians there told me a tale which was surely untrue.

A black musician, who was a Hendrix look-alike, had arrived to record. During his session, he suddenly broke into a superb guitar solo, as good as the recently dead Hendrix at his best. He emerged from the sound-stage grey and shaking, asking what had happened....had he passed out? No, was the reply, he had recorded a brilliant track....but when the tapes were played back....they were blank!

Now this is a folktale, of the kind that people scoff at yet still tell with conviction about all kinds of subjects. It is also a folktale in a modern professional context, emerging in a very hard businesslike world. Like many folktales, it was only transferred to a limited group or family, and did not ever achieve more than local currency. It was limited to its own professional 'village', in exactly the same way that old rituals, superstitions or songs were regionally confined in the past. Like these localised sources of folklore, our sample story uses basic images and patterns which we know were part of actual pagan religious belief and usage. The elements present are 1. superstitious 2. magical 3. mythical. These three divisions are matters of degree, or level of awareness, and usually merge into one another in any folktale or drama.

The superstitious element lies in fact that the recording machines could not record the music (assuming that the studio crew were not idiots who forgot to do their jobs properly). This is typical superstition in modern context, where the technology of this world cannot register the events of the Otherworld.

3

The magical element, which is connected to the superstitious, begins where the musician was 'a double' for the dead Hendrix, and then played 'exactly like him'. This is quite primitive magic, where the spirit of a dead hero or ancestor takes over the body of a living relative, apprentice, or double in some way or other, usually for the purposes of prophecy.

On a mythical level, the hero in the Otherworld had inspired the mere mortal to superhuman flights of creativity. Our musician was apparently taking part in a typical pagan experience, uplifted by the god-like image of the dead star. We even call our most successful and beloved entertainers '*stars*' because the ancients believed that the spirits of dead heroes or heroines became as stars in the night sky....a star is an elevated or highly placed being.

As I said earlier, the tale is surely untrue, (although everyone who told it believed it at the time), yet its blatant untruth does not in any way affect its value as a myth....particularly in the heightened atmosphere of loss generated by the death of a modern hero. Furthermore, the story has a *real* value that reaches out from its shadowy content, for it says "look to the talent and skill of those who have tried before you, if they can do it, *you* can do it. Learn from them, be inspired by them:...but don't ever think that real inspiration and magic can ever be tamed....or taped!".

Our explanation of the example is by no means idle or speculative. The ancients were particularly concerned with 'the Ancestors' the 'Otherworld' and the means of communication between our outer realm and the inner ones. The system was not similar to modern spiritism (spiritualism) but was based upon more mature foundations, with deep philosophical aspects which have guided modern religion and science through their course towards the present era.

The Celts were involved in a cult-of-the-dead....and British mythology is mainly derived from Celtic sources. Actual examples of Celtic myth are numerous, but available interpretations vary in aim and quality, and are often highly prejudiced by religious belief. One of the most frequent problems encountered by the reader of any series or collection of British myths is that the material appears to be confusing, diffuse, and incoherent; unlike Classical myths which can be referred to a central pantheon of gods and goddesses. The Celtic pantheon certainly exists, but not in the regular manner defined by classical studies.

The diffusion referred to exists for several reasons. First, the actual source material is often garbled and obscure, as much of it derives from fragments set down in the middle ages, when much of the old lore was being deliberately or accidentally forgotten. Other elements are derived from oral tradition, from tales in which all but the bare bones have been eroded away by time. Secondly, a great number of the pagan practices and tales were ruthlessly and bloodily suppressed, so it is rather remarkable that so much *has* survived, in any form at all.

Early researchers, mainly in the 19th century, had very little to work on that was recognisably 'Celtic', and were limited by the conditioning of their social status and a Christian and classical education. This educational restriction tended to colour translation and research, editing and presentation of British myth. It is only in the recent years that strict new translations of early Welsh, Irish, Scottish and medieval pagan tales in general have begun to appear for intelligent commentary and careful re-assessment.

Finally, there is another and major problem. British mythology *is* diffuse! It was not connected to a central cult, or a major god or goddess with specific worship centres and rules of behaviour or ritual. This concept may be particularly difficult for us to grasp, for we are used to the centralised Christian worship and dogma, which was derived from the Roman political state worship that it absorbed.

The British gods and goddesses are numerous, and very colourful, but there was no defined hierarchy, or even 'religion' in the modern sense of the words. To understand this non-system, we have to remember that pagan worship was environmental, and that each sacred place had its own god, goddess or power. In Britain these were very local indeed, hardly moving from their regular sites and habitual homes. To merely make a list, therefore, of deities in Britain, or even in the wider Celtic realms of Europe, is only to add to the confusion. Statistical and rational analysis may not hold good throughout, for many deities occur only once, while others occur frequently, but with differing attributes. Some, mercifully, remain fairly constant, but these are not necessarily the main powers of our hypothetical Celtic pantheon.

The value of myth is that it offers keys to understanding, often to understanding of many different types or aspects of knowledge at once. To the ancients the value of such keys was invested in ritual, where magic was made in accordance with observed signs and seasons and places, and was thought to bring fertility and benefit from the Otherworld to human and animal recipients. Even the above is something of a simplification of the purpose of ritual, but it serves as a loose definition for our present context, giving some of the main 'aims' of the pagan holistic world-view.

Nowadays we do not hold such beliefs, but the keys can still work to unlock areas of awareness long neglected, shadowy and shut, to let the light into them for our own benefit. Myths can still give meaning and pattern to life, and are not in conflict with a modern or religious attitude. Most science and religion is upheld by its own mythology in any case.

The best way to come to grips with the slippery British myth is to grasp the root elements of it. These hold good throughout all myth and folklore, and can be used to define and correlate apparently obscure examples into a system of reference. The system is not rigid, however, for it is based upon a cycle, or spiral, a pattern which is derived originally from seasonal worship. We can expect it to go around and around, but be different every time it recommences....like the flow of the years themselves.

To produce a theoretical method for understanding the connective elements in British mythology is not enough. Such a theory has to be supported by a mass of literary evidence ranging through numerous special fields of study, which make considerable demands upon the reader....not the least of which is that of time. Anyone who has read any of the famous works on folklore or myth will know just *how* demanding such studies are!

There is another way to approach the problem, a way by which the reader can establish some firm concepts, some essential central keys which link the ancient world with the myths and tales handed down from various sources. We can use a model....and there is a very good example of a British site, combined with classical Roman and Greek elements, which shows the principle areas of native myth and worship in practice. If the evidence from this site, Aquae Sulis, is combined with literary and folklore material relating to its physical remains as uncovered by archaeology, a model of mythology in practice can be built up. This model may be used, with care and caution, as a comparative example for study of un-sited British myths, or of other less researched and less well documented sites.

The use of Aquae Sulis as the model is not random, for it is one of the most striking, most complete and best documented sites known in Britain, and the visible remains are from a period well suited for evidence and comparison, that of the Roman development of the West Country of England; when Celtic culture and Roman civilisation merged together and produced a flowering of symbolic and inscriptive material in the Temple and baths around the Hot Springs.

Myths have a curious habit of standing values upon their heads, of sudden reversals and rapid changes of fortune for obscure reasons once thought of as the whims of the gods and goddesses by later mis-interpretors of the pagan viewpoint. Some of these reasons are revealed in the following pages, which, like the myths themselves, have an intertwined multiple value, for they are a study of the mythology of one specific and remarkable place in Britain, yet also offer keys to the themes of British lore in general, and to the less obvious or transparent secrets of overall mythology.

There are two main characters in the tale; the goddess Sulis-Minerva, in whose Temple burnt an Eternal Flame, and her "son", or protected hero, Bladud, who was a mythical king of Britain and like the Sun itself flew through the upper air on wings. So direct and widespread are these two images, that we can trace their pattern to a parallel from an earlier culture, that of Egypt....but this is not to suggest that the Egyptian counterparts were in any way the originals, for such myths flower independantly wherever there are people.

The Goddess Neitha, a Weaver, was often identified by the Greeks with their goddess Athena. Athena became, in time, the Roman Minerva, to whom the Temple of Sulis Minerva (at Bath, England) was partly dedicated. The main centre of worship for Neitha was at Säis in Lower Egypt, and during her annual festival, innumerable lamps were kept alight in her honour. The Classical writers Plutarch and Proclus both state that her temple bore the following inscription: "I AM ALL THAT HAS BEEN, THAT IS, AND THAT WILL BE: AND NO MAN HATH LIFTED MY VEIL. THE SUN WAS MY CHILD".

Aquae Sulis
The Waters of The Gap
The Author's Preface

I have lived over the Roman Baths of Aquae Sulis for ten years, literally over the central area, close to where the Hot Springs arise, and where the Baths and Temple were built during the Roman period. From the top of my house, I can look down into the waters of the Great Bath, and on winter mornings the steam from the main spring and the baths blows over my roof garden. Living within the ancient and hallowed centre with its therapeutic waters, an entire progression of cultural strata from the Roman period through to the adjoining Abbey then on to the Georgian housing and finally the modern city, it is surely no wonder that I have developed a deep interest in the origins of my adopted home.

In my period of living in Bath, I have researched and written several books and articles, made many musical recordings, and filmed and broadcast from the Pump Rooms and Roman Baths themselves. This particular book began in 1970, when I made my first visit to the museum, and has been the cause of subsequent years of research and study, drawing strands together from many widespread and differing sources.

I should state immediately that I am not an archaeologist, and that I have relied entirely on the archaeological resources of the authorities on the site....particularly the work of Professor Cunliffe. Furthermore, I have no intention of adding to, or arguing with, any of the major archaeological studies of Aquae Sulis. My approach has been from a quite different viewpoint, which has incorporated archaeological evidence with traditional lore, medieval manuscript material, and our ever increasing knowledge and re-assessment of the cultures of the past....knowledge which is derived from many sources, including cultural anthropology, folklore, history, linguistic evidence, literary history, and the study of the development of magic and religion from most primitive roots to complex ritual and philosophy.

In many ways my work has been much easier than that of the archaeologist, as it has been possible to draw on 'absolutes', known patterns of cultural development and ancient practice and belief, and then point out the supportive evidence. The basic theories that are suggested here will hold good, even when the archaeological work is far in advance of its present state. It has already progressed since this book was first conceived and written, and the sheer volume of work waiting for the experts is considerable. For that reason alone, it seems worth contributing a general study of the mythology and traditional lore associated with Aquae Sulis....something that bridges the gap between the detailed archaeological work and the many theoretical studies of ancient times that are available to the reader, and furthermore shows how general cultural and religious patterns were particularly manifest in one place.

In the pursuit of such a synthesis, I have fallen over several curious pieces of knowledge, all readily available and accessible, but in widely separated sources. In some cases, as in the writings of Professor Sayce discussed in the text, I found that my own research had already been anticipated by earlier theorists....but *they* had not had the benefit of the excellent archaeological studies published in recent years, so lacked detailed supportive evidence and the broader point of view which modern developments have generated. Particularly relevant to this discussion is the difference between the 'classical' education, which was prevalent until early years this century, and the 'modern' education which has now largely replaced it. Many of the important analyses of ancient sites are strongly influenced by a central 'classicism' in which all material is related to Greek or Roman examples. While present-day archaeologists are generally free of this culturally limiting attitude, their immediate forebears and authorities definitely were not, and should be read with their educational and religious backgrounds firmly in mind. Furthermore, as popular report is always a generation or more behind developed research, I have felt it worthwhile to examine and explain in detail the reasons for several *apparent* errors or conflicts in the study of Aquae Sulis that have appeared in print....in the hope that the reader will understand that they are *not* really errors or conflicts at all but merely differences in expression of the same set of facts.

No archaeologist would argue that the Baths were frequented by Italians or actual residents of the city of Rome, arriving in great numbers....for they had far more exotic and developed bathing places of their own. Yet the popular image, derived from early research into the site, is that Aquae Sulis was the sporting place of toga-draped Romans from Rome, speaking pure Latin.

Although all free-born inhabitants were Roman citizens after the year 214 A.D., and despite the fact that Latin was widely spoken in Britain, the native Celtic element of the temple site is very strong indeed. This is not a unique situation, however, for such local elements were commonplace throughout the Empire....and were in fact the rule rather than exceptions.

Also significant of a native importance to the site, is the strong possibility suggested in the medieval chronicles that Aquae Sulis has a British and Celtic solar myth connected to its Temple of Minerva.

A serious consideration of this myth, which has many widespread parallels in ancient cultures, and is further complemented by a typical folk-tale collected in the late 17th century, sheds a fresh light on the interpretation of the remains recovered from the Roman period, particularly the world famous Roman/Celtic carvings which were associated with worship. To come to an understanding of the relevance of much of this material, I felt it necessary to deal with the very essential roots of a site such as the hot springs....the environmental and primitive worship which was the basis for the sophisticated Roman developments. By doing so, I hope to have demonstrated the *continuity* and *integration* of the symbolism of the remains and the actual nature of the site itself....to have shown that there is really no question of interpretative conflict between a 'Celtic' or a 'Roman' reading of the evidence. After all, the people who *built* the place seem to have achieved some kind of mutual cultural integration, otherwise we simply would not have such a wealth of evidence to consider!

I do not subscribe to any of the wilder romantic theories about Celts and Druids that have been associated with Bath, particularly by 18th century antiquarians, and which have in turn influenced modern popular writing and folk-lore within our society.

Writing fantasies about the Druids is by no means a modern occupation, for classical authors, including Julius Caesar, set the scene while the Druids themselves were still operating in Gaul and Britain. Some of the 'popular press' from Roman sources has been shown to be physically impossible....such as the burning of human sacrifices in wicker baskets....but other aspects of Druidic wisdom are still being debated today, supported by factual evidence such as the Coligny Calendar which shows sophisticated powers of observation of lunar and solar cycles. Although we have no proof in the shape of archaeological evidence, it is certain that the Celtic worship around the hot springs would have involved the Druids, possibly replaced by a more Romanised priesthood during the 1st century A.D.

At Aquae Sulis, the archaeologists have revealed remarkable remains. This book offers an analysis of the mythical and magical elements of those remains, which I trust will still be seen, touched, and further opened out in years to come.

BATH. 1980.

"The Celts" at Aquae Sulis

The terms 'Celt' and 'Celtic' are used in the broadest historical and cultural sense within this study of pagan symbolism at Aquae Sulis. It is certain that Greece and Rome shared many aspects of their heritage with the Celts....but over a long period of time they were established civilisations, while the Celts were still 'barbaric'.

The Celts who sacked Rome in 387 B.C. were not city dwellers, nor were they builders in stone. The centuries of conflict between Romans and Celts were not entirely a matter of Imperial growth, nor one of racial expansion and migration....although these are the primary rationalisations of the history of their relationship. The Celtic peoples retained a primitive and fluid outlook, shown clearly in their mythology and non-organisation; while the Romans had developed as masters of structure and moulding of *civilisation* in the strictest sense, that of society based upon a city centralised system. By the 1st century B.C. some Celtic tribes were organised as states with an urban base, but this was far removed from the degree of organisation of Rome and the Empire.

This 'difference', the hallmark of Celtic peoples, can still be felt today in the traditional and cultural heritage of the natives of Ireland, Scotland, Wales and Brittany....though it has travelled many devious routes from the origins of the head-hunting spirit-worshipping ancestors. It should not be forgotten, that this 'Celtic' spirit and imagination actually helped to retain civilisation during the Dark Ages, when the structure established by Rome was finally swept aside by a new influx of barbarism. The interplay between 'Roman' and 'Celt' is actually long and complex....and should never be encapsulated or romanticised when considering the history of Britain and Europe. There were many tribes and nations of Celts, and they fought with each other just as frequently as they battled with Romans, Greeks or Macedonians....or any other people that they came into contact with!

There was little or no political unity among the Celts, in the modern or Roman sense of the words....but there was a distinctive flow of cultural entity, held together by specific imaginative and symbolic elements. It is material of this sort that is clearly recognisable at Aquae Sulis, merged with its Roman and Greek counterparts.

The long perspective of Celtic histories should be pursued in the many excellent books available, some of which are listed in the following pages. The details given above are mere examples of a complex and often obscure subject, which has suffered from intentional mystification at one extreme of romantic imaginative restoration, and from considerable suppression and over-rationalisation at the other extreme, through derision of pre-Roman cultures in Europe as a matter of general policy.

'The Celts' may be defined historicaly, archaeologically, and by cross reference to the classical descriptions available to us. They may be defined linguistically from early inscriptions, and by derivation of place and proper names. Most important of all, they may be recognised by specific themes of mythical and magical material....which evolved from a primitive death and ancestor cult, through to the mystical Christian allegory of the Holy Grail, which appeared in written form in the 13th century.

The Celtic contribution to Aquae Sulis should not be thought of as an imaginative correction to the excessive 'Romanisation' of local history. The vitality and power of the native imagination merged with the Roman talent for discipline and structure....those very elements that the Celts have often lacked. These two cultural streams, *together*, made Aquae Sulis; there is no question of Romans building the site out of nothing and bestowing it upon savages, nor of wildly creative and mystical Celts re-vivifying stodgy and materialistic Romans. Writers who tend towards either of these extremes are probably expressing aspects of their own personalities and limitations, and simply have not looked twice at the mass of evidence available....once for the Romans, and once for the Celts!

The Celts referred to in connection with The Temple and Baths of Aquae Sulis were a mixture of loosely related peoples. They had a common stock of life-symbols in worship, and a common linguistic ground, some of which is apparent in native languages of the present day, such as Irish, Welsh, Gaelic and Breton. Some proof of this linguistic material is suggested by the chronicles that discuss Bath in British mythological terms, while relating native language names to the classical temple, and these chronicles were first written out as late as the 12th or 13th century. In addition we have inscriptions from the Roman period that clearly use Celtic language words combined with Latin.

The people that produced this cultural heritage, with its own clearly identifiable spirit, were by no means a *civilisation*, yet they had a high level of culture, and tremendous imaginative and artistic ability, combined with well defined social and religious patterns of behaviour.

There are still many conflicting and difficult matters of evidence, when we consider the Celtic element of the material at Bath. We know, from classical writers, that Celtic society was powerfully influenced by the Druids, who seem to have travelled freely and been the source of a great deal of agitation and retaliation against Roman rule. Druidism was proscribed by the Empire, and the native gods and goddesses gradually appeared in Roman-ised forms, such as those found at Aquae Sulis. Yet while our site was being developed, Druids still held sway in nearby Wales, and revolts in south-east England caused the natives to revert to human sacrifice. Was Aquae Sulis therfore an entirely *political* temple site, a deliberate means of containing a rebellious and potentially savage people by demonstrating the suppression of their own gods by those of Rome? Or was it a site of such religious or magical significance that both forms of worship would be merged without discomfort, and people could travel to it for bathing, therapy and prophecy without fear of discord?

The present author tends towards the second theory, which is more in keeping with the deeper aspects of pagan belief in general, and was perpetuated well into the Middle Ages, when Christian sanctuaries were regarded as being outside the rule of temporal authorities, a direct inheritance of the inviolability of the ancient temple sites. It may be that future excavation will reveal more information regarding the *aims* of the site, particularly in connection with the native populace. Meanwhile we must be content with the overall mythical and magical elements of the Celtic worship and its Roman counterparts, analysed in the following pages.

Sources of Information

The Roman Baths at Bath are situated in one of the best preserved groups of early Roman-British remains in England. Although the site is world famous as "the Roman Baths", it actually combines a Roman style bathing complex with a sacred Spring enclosure and a Temple building in a classical style that has native influences. In addition to these known buildings, there are others of uncertain use, and at least one other religious spring site (The Cross Bath) all grouped around the Hot Springs which still rise within the centre of the modern city. The remains have been the subject of a great deal of research since the first phase of rediscovery in the late eighteenth century, and they are well documented and described in modern archaeological terms. At first glance, it might seem unnecessary to add another book to those already available on Aquae Sulis, or to write more about the site until fresh excavations bring new solid material to light. No short summary of the religious and magical basis of the site has ever been made however, so this analysis makes a supplement to the major works written for serious students, and can also be used as a guide when looking at the remains themselves.

Aquae Sulis was undoubtedly developed because of the pagan belief in the power of springs, and the abundant flow and high natural temperature of the waters would have enhanced this reverance in various ways evident from the dedications and carvings recovered from excavation. There are some vital links between modern archaeological evidence and ancient patterns of behaviour as described by the classical and post-classical writers who dealt with the religious, magical and cultural influences of their day. Several strands of information have been brought together in this book, which have previously been kept separate with regard to Aquae Sulis. A comparison of known history, myth, folklore and traditional history can be made with the visible remains from the area of the Hot Springs, and this gives us a direct and unusual insight into the minds of the people who lived, bathed and worshipped there. Such an insight helps to bring the fragmented remains to life, and adds a new dimension of interest, particularly for the non-archaeologist or general enthusiast who is interested in the early cultures, but unfamiliar with the mass of technical and architectural description found in the major works which are available.

To bring Aquae Sulis into a fresh perspective, we should compare literary and archaeological sources, both classical and native British. The physical remains relate in many ways to information given in famous classical writings, such as those of Julius Caesar, Pliny, Sotion, Diogenes Laertius, Tacitus and others. These ancient authors, surviving in texts ranging from complete works to fragmented quotations, span a long period of time, and all have comments and facts to offer us about the world in which they lived. Their information can be compared to various details and patterns connected with the site of the Hot Springs of Aquae Sulis, and we can gradually build a picture of the cultural attitudes which make such a site grow and prosper.

Another important literary source comes from Britain, in the form of a group of chronicles or mythical histories which contain direct references to Bath. These chronicles are not true histories, but hold within themselves a colourful collection of distorted folk tales, myths, and other material, which can be traced to pagan origins, and in the movements and migrations of various races across Europe, remembered in mythical form.

The main source of these tales is Geoffrey of Monmouth, a 12th century Welsh historian and churchman. He drew material from the popular tradition of his day, and from other written sources available to him, such as the chronicle of Tysilio, also of Welsh origin; Nennius; the work of Solinus, writing in the third century A.D.; and according to Geoffrey himself, a manuscript source brought from Brittany for him to render into Latin from the old British or Welsh tongue with which he was naturally familiar. The actual existence of this book has been debated by critics and scholars since Geoffrey's day....and is discussed in greater detail later in our text.

The elements of Geoffrey's stories are very similar to various Irish, Welsh, Scots and Breton folk tales, many of which reflect early pagan customs and beliefs. These stories give us an insight into the Celtic 'magical' attitude to life, and into various social and cultural patterns derived from pagan times. As the West of England was occupied by these same Celts, (and the descendants of the earlier peoples whom the Celts had absorbed) at exactly the time of the Roman development of the Hot Springs, an examination of their beliefs is very valuable, and clarifies many details about the site which at first seem to be obscure, contradictory, or even unknown through any other sources.

For many years, the old chronicles were sneered at by serious historians, and reckoned to be ignorant, or downright dishonest. Such an opinion is correct from the viewpoint of literal factual history....which seeks to establish *exact* records and dates for the sequence of past events, often with great difficulty. But it is not correct when the seemingly absurd old tales are examined for evidence relating symbolically or mythically to the past. The Chronicles derive a great deal of their contents from well preserved oral traditions, which are strongly conservative in process, and retain all sorts of elements from pre-Christian and essentially pre-literary cultures. Because of this strong aversion to changing any of the old tales, which are quite illogical by anyone's usual standard of common sense, the fabulous histories and geneologies remained intact for a very long time, through several centuries of copying and printing.

In recent years, the response of historians and archaeologists to traditional material has altered considerably and there is a greater tendency to allow for and analyse the accuracy of oral and folk tales set down at various times through history.

Of particular value are the definable myths and folktales written out at early dates, such as those of Geoffrey and other British writers who preserved native lore.

We should not be too surprised to find that the old tales which mention Bath correspond in several ways to the research of the modern archaeologists. Geoffrey mentions the existence of a Temple of Minerva, but during his time the Temple was lost beneath the mud and silt from the centuries of flooding, after the abandoning of the site in the late Roman-British period. He was obviously drawing from an earlier source of information, that of Solinus, combined with the traditional material of Celtic origin, with which he was very familiar. Geoffrey worked his traditional material into a very unlikely geneology of the Kings of Britain, and included King Bladud as the founder of the City of Bath and of the Temple. This statement seems at first to be in complete conflict with the archaeological evidence, but can be related to it very well indeed.

Serious archaeological work on the site of Aquae Sulis has always been difficult, as it is right in the middle of a busy modern city, and by a curious twist of fate, the very magnificence and fascination of the remains draws an immense number of visitors each year, making work on further revelations extremely limited. Professor Barry Cunliffe, the authority on the Roman remains at Bath, also points out some of the more subtle difficulties, in his preface to "Roman Bath" published by the Society of Antiquaries in 1969.

.....“The blame must rest not with the relative inaccessability of the monuments themselves, nor with the archaeologists who have visited them, but with the physical atmosphere of the town, for on arrival a distinctive lethargy descends and one becomes cocooned in the slow sticky air, barely capable of physical exertion and totally unable to indulge in constructive thought. The only answer is to commute daily from as far afield as possible. It may be that some succumb more easily than others; Francis Haverfield, however, having grown up in the town, became acclimatized and was able, with characteristic industry, to produce his masterly survey of the Roman settlement and its remains for the ‘Victoria County History’ which has remained a standard work to the present day. But after that, with the notable exception of the pioneer work of W.H. Knowles, the archaeology of the town lay dormant until Sir Ian Richmond began his patient and elegant exploration of the East Baths in 1954” (*Cunliffe, preface, Roman Bath*).

Despite the problems and despite the undisputed fact that there is still a lot to be uncovered, there is sufficient evidence around the central spring to draw basic conclusions, which are supported by the classical and early British references, and by comparison to other British and Continental examples of similar sites. Apparently fantastic folk tales will be found to be as factual as the stones left by the Romans, once both are correctly interpreted.

Most of the remains excavated to date are on show to the public, and various other artifacts and fragments from the locality are added to the museum next to the Great Bath. Not all of the material on show comes from the central spring region, and it tends to show that the entire complex extended over an area similar to that of the old city boundaries. Most of the remains, both small and monumental, can be seen on or close to their place of origin, which makes the site a fascinating and highly popular one to visit. Millions of people have gazed in wonder at the stone-carved head that once guarded the entrance to the Temple. This image is still intact, 1800 years or more after its carving, and is one of the most striking examples of the magical-head symbolism in British pagan tradition. It can be paired with the relief carving of the head and shoulders of a lunar goddess, also well preserved, but less dynamic and lavish in style, which is shown nearby.

Still impressive today is the dark steaming vault where the natural hot water flows out on its way to the River Avon. What could have prompted the ancient people to worship in this place? Why did they carve the head, and the numerous other images....?

A primitive impulse, that originated somewhere in the unknown past, connected closely with the flow of the apparently endless hot waters, eventually grew into the complex and massive development of religious and therapeutic buildings which we can appreciate from the recent years of excavation. If the visitor to the source has the rare opportunity to stand alone for a few moments inside the vault where the waters issue from the spring and reservoir, he or she might feel something of that same mysterious power that motivated early people to worship in such places.

It all began with a simple urge to relate to the powers of the earth and water, which were thought to be the obvious source of all living things. To begin to understand the Roman-British remains, we must first consider how such drives towards nature worship were a root and essential part of the way of life of the ancients, both Roman and non-Roman alike.

The physical dimensions and historical possibilities of the monuments available for study at present have been described by the writers mentioned above. Cunliffe's 'Roman Bath' is the main archaeological reference work used in this study, and the technical details are not repeated, except where they have any direct significance to the cultural or magical/religious roots being discussed.

The main emphasis of the archaeological studies has been on the Baths themselves, and the general technical description of the monumental architecture. The religious and mythical elements of Aquae Sulis have never been co-ordinated, although their importance has been repeatedly acknowledged.

Our present knowledge of primitive religion, and its later evolved pagan stages, suggests that reverence of a mother goddess, at the source of the hot waters, created the focus from which grew all the sophisticated developments of the Roman period. This can be demonstrated by the symbols used in the carvings, and the context of the inscriptions, when compared to other known pagan sites and practices. We cannot re-establish the fine details of the ritual workings native to Aquae Sulis, but there is still an immense body of information which survives intact from the classical sources dealing with both Greek, Roman and Celtic worship, much of which would be contemporary with the period of three or four centuries in which the Baths were used or at least accessible.

The importance of the hot springs themselves can be traced to a pre-Roman phase, mainly Celtic, directly in keeping with pagan worship in Europe prior to the growth of the Empire. Before examining the details of the carvings, dedications, and structural evidence in detail, and before comparing these to the written sources that mention Bath, we should first examine the basis of belief from which they all grew.

The Three Mothers

Pagan Nature and Spring Worship

In York Street, which runs above the site of the Roman Baths, there is a plaque which tells us that "These Hot Springs were used by the Romans as early as the First Century. In area, in grandeur, in completeness, the Baths of Aquae Sulis were unequalled".

This proud statement is no exaggeration as far as Britain is concerned, for Aquae Sulis was a specially developed site with no similar major hot springs comparable anywhere else in the country.

The growth of this group of buildings is even more striking and suggestive than might at first be thought, for they were not at the heart of the civilised Empire, nor in one of the well developed Provinces that had their own cities and major baths. Aquae Sulis was one of the most distant corners of a distant outpost, on an island that was never fully incorporated into the Empire.

The city itself was close to the wild Welsh regions, which harboured the savage people who had come to Britain long before the Romans....people whose ancestors had sacked Rome herself at one time. These 'untamed' Celts were never integrated into the Empire, unlike the Celts of Gaul, but remained independant, until their religious sanctuary on Mona (Anglesey) was destroyed during the 1st century; and probably for a long period after that. Hardly a promising beginning for a civilised and sophisticated bathing spot!

Yet the buildings of Aquae Sulis were reworked and improved upon over a long period of time, during which Southern and part of Western England was more or less under the Roman peace, and they attracted people from many parts of the Empire, as the inscriptions show. The city was not a military stronghold, but seems to have had an almost entirely religious development with the later trading and social benefits attached to its growth as a worship site on a route-centre.

The importance of the place, to Roman and to non-Roman alike, was rooted in the hot springs. The central elements of the site are the Springs, the Temple and the Baths, dedicated to the goddess Sulis, with various other deities or powers attached and loosely related in the typical pagan manner. The design of the building with the 'Gorgon's Head' upon its pediment was typical of a native worship site under strong classical influence; its Greek and Roman style combined with Celtic symbolism suggest that it may be a replacement or addition to an existing worship site.

The blending of Roman and native worship was partly due to the political attempts at 'Romanising', which were applied in varying degrees to most subject races. The process included a deliberate absorbing of native cults into the official religions, yet it also worked the other way around as Rome took up various religions and cults that arrived through the expansion of the Empire. The ultimately successful cult was, of course, Christianity. Emperor worship was developed and encouraged as a controlling device, and traces of this are evident in the inscriptions at Bath.

On a broader scale, however, this exchange and absorption process is typical of the evolution of religion, where cults and beliefs grow and merge with each other, through military conquest, trade, and the exchanges of knowledge and craftsmanship connected with trading activities. During the growth of Christian influence, for example, many of the early saints are thin disguises for pagan gods and goddesses, the victims of an immense spiritual take-over bid.

An important point, usually overlooked by modern people, is that the overall pagan attitude seems to have been one of religious tolerance. The Romans probably absorbed this attitude from the Greeks, and only completely destroyed native temples when the people who built them were politically intolerable and troublesome. Both the Jews and the Druids, two quite different fanatical cults which caused the Empire problems, had their sanctuaries destroyed.

This general degree of tolerance was changed by Christianity when it finally became the Roman state religion, as it developed an aggressive attitude towards all other cults which it determined to destroy. The gods and goddesses named at Aquae Sulis should be thought of in the context of this broad pre-Christian religious tolerance, but it was not a philanthropic tolerance based upon any kind of benign concept. A close look at the pagan gods and goddesses will show that they were all broadly linked together by common attributes, and were recognisable and adaptable from race to race and culture to culture. They were examples of regional fertility worship at their most local, and derived from broadly disseminated recognition of basic life and death powers at their most international, levels.

All this should be borne in mind when thinking about the worship at Bath, but the main feature, the truly important feature, was the abundant flow of hot water from several springs. Springs were always revered and worshipped in the pagan world, and were seen as focus points for the power of the earth, at which gods and goddesses dwelt, and from which power and blessing flowed. They were thought to be clear and simple evidence of the abundance of the mother earth, and at major spring sites successive races and groups merged together, and evolved long and complex traditions of worship. Perhaps the most famous of such sites was the oracle at Delphi, which is comparable symbolically to the site at Aquae Sulis. This oracle was a "sacred-centre" of the ancient world, and was under the patronage of Appollo the sun god, who controlled music, healing, sanity, and the passage of the Sun itself. He was supposed to have taken up residence there after killing a serpent (possibly a totem beast of an earlier goddess cult) which originally belonged within. One major feature of Delphi was a cave, where a priestess went into a prophetic trance by breathing the fumes that emerged from below, after first bathing in a sacred spring. These spring and cavern elements are fundamental to the development of religious thought in all primitive cultures, and were refined to great complexity and sophistication in the pre-Christian religions. People were prompted to worship in such places by very strong and simple urges connected with life and death, and the subsequent attributes of each individual site grew from such basic beginnings.

Any understanding of the remains of pagan worship places should *not* start with the gods and goddesses themselves, though this is normally the manner in which such sites are analysed. The deities are later attributes, derived from totem animals and ancestor worship, in a subtle progression of symbolic evolution. Understanding must start with a firm grasp of the concept of the 'Otherworld', a concept of such underlying importance that all magical and religious thought was derived from it, and which is inherent in the choice and in the structure of the pagan worship sites themselves. Yet this same concept is the most readily overlooked or rationalised by modern writers and readers, as it has been almost totally abandoned in contemporary thought and education. This altering of attitude has fortunate aspects also, for it has liberated us from the suppressive control of religion and enables us to look anew at the pagan concepts without conditioned prejudices.

The pagan Otherworld was a world beyond death, and features strongly in all magic and religion. There is a large difference between the pagan Otherworld, and the later Christian concepts of "Heaven and Hell". The Otherworld was effective, it was a seething and dynamic source of energy and life, a realm from which all possible benefits, including human life itself, were derived. Conversely, it was also the place of death, the land to which all return, and the secret place from which the spirits of the dead operated. This concept of the apparent duality of the Otherworld was natural to the pagan mind, and is beautifuly illustrated by the story of Peredur, a Welsh myth derived from native Celtic tradition.

'Peredur rode on towards a river valley whose edges were forested, with level meadows on both sides of the river; on one bank there was a flock of white sheep, and on the other a flock of black sheep. When a white sheep bleated a black sheep would cross the river and turn white, and when a black sheep bleated a white sheep would cross the river and turn black. On the bank of the river he saw a tall tree; from roots to crown one half was aflame, and the other green with leaves....' (*The Mabinogion, trans. Jeffrey Gantz, Penguin*). In the Christian expositions of the Otherworld, its balanced duality has become total separation, with Heaven and Hell battling for supremacy and the possession of the human soul. The pagan concept, as outlined in the extract from Peredur, was that life and death, positive and negative, were balanced aspects of one whole picture. The exchange of the sheep across the river dividing the two worlds illustrates this, as does the dual nature of the tree, which has the green leaves of the natural environment, and the magical flames of the Otherworld.

The Otherworld concept was initially identified with an Earth mother, a fertility and death goddess, and so all springs and caves were the obvious visible signs of her nature and bounty. Myths are full of tales about journeys to or from the Otherworld, which is under the ground, under or over water, or associated with a cave spring or well entrance. Thinking of this sort grows quite simply from a direct observation of nature. Such observation was originally essential for basic day to day survival, but in time it developed into a code of patterns of ritual behaviour linked to natural phenomena such as the seasons of the year, the growth of plants, the migration of animals, and the occasions of hunting and farming that went with them. The ancients had a quite different sense of relationship to the environment, different from that of modern man, and different again from that instilled in the

Christian era, when nature was regarded as an enemy or delusional snare for the senses.

The seasonal observations were important to both hunting and agriculture, and were further developed into accurate observations of the passage of the moon, sun and plants, and some of the visible stars. Modern research has begun to prove that the ancient people had developed a rather surprising accuracy in this study of the sky, the forerunner of both astrology and its child, astronomy. Some of the stone circles and alignments in Britain are built upon such observations, and their construction dates back long before the Celts first appeared.

The basis of this concern with observing the environment was that all life and death followed a pattern, a pattern which the observer could eventually discern and ultimately relate to in order to obtain maximum benefit. The simplest form of this pattern was the cycle of the seasons, which could be seen through plants, the movements of animals and the weather, and was assumed to apply also to mankind.

All things were thought to have their birth at Spring, their Summer when they flourished, their Autumn of maturity and fruitfulness, and then the Winter of repose and death. Because plants were seen to die back into the earth and become reborn the following Spring, so were animals and men and women thought to follow the same cycle. Very primitive people generally think that mankind emerged from the earth itself, and even the Christians retained a creation myth of this sort; "And the Lord God formed man of the dust of the ground, and breathed into his nostrils the breath of life", (*Genesis,2,7*). In popular superstition and folklore the fairies or Otherworld beings lived in hollow hills, or underground, and were often indistinguishable from the ancestral spirits of the dead. Indeed, this earth conception retained its popularity well into the Middle Ages and later, when learned men were debating about the spontaneous generation of life from dunghills, and the main bulk of the Christian faithful were expecting or arguing about a *bodily* resurrection for all at the second coming of Christ, when corpses would leap out of their graves and the elect be physically taken up to Heaven. These concepts seem silly to the modern scientifically educated reader, but once they are seen in context they are definable as direct descendants of the pagan world-Otherworld picture in a somewhat debased and misguided form.

From the information that has survived, the written descriptions of beliefs and the myths themselves, we can conclude that the pagans regarded death as a return to the source of life; the Other or Spirit World. The Celts, as the classical writers tell us, had what appears to the modern eye to be an obsession with synchronicity and derived ritual actions, but evidence of the same magical actions is clear in the Roman state rituals, lessened by the nature of their urban civilisation.

The idea of death as the return to the source of life is deceptively simple, and it leads to several important conclusions that can be seen very clearly within the symbolism of the Temple and other buildings at Aquae Sulis. Even the social bathing, which is generally assumed to be the reason for Bath's fame in Roman times, was originally linked to magical and religious functions. Where the waters are used for purification and therapy there is little to help us make any clear distinction between religious/magical use, and the social developments attendant upon large numbers of people gathering in a special place.

From the concept of physical death as a return to the Otherworld, from which all life comes, many distinct ritual patterns and educational processes were worked out and put into action. These originated with simple actions connected with life activities such as battle or hunting, and were often intended to do nothing more than trick or appease the spirits of the dead. In time they developed into rituals which were supposed to help humans make the transition from one world to another, and also to help them bring back the benefits from the Otherworld.

The best known examples of highly developed systems of this sort are probably the Egyptian so-called "Book of the Dead", and the stunning monuments of ancient Egypt itself. The Classical examples are the various "Mysteries", which included the Elusinian, the Orphic, and the mysteries of Isis, derived from Egypt.

A Mystery was basically a type of school, which offered education, and a graded series of initiations which were supposed to go beyond the mass levels of public worship. The Roman army, for example, is known to have favoured the mystery of Mithras which was of Persian origin. Many of the features of Christianity were taken from this Mystery, particularly the organisational patterns and the solar symbolism. The Celts had the famous Druidic mysteries, about which a great deal of nonsense has been written from Roman times right up to the present day. Julius Caesar tells us that the Druid cult originated in Britain, and that students travelled there from Europe for advanced study during his lifetime. He also tells us that the main doctrine of the Druids was that "souls do not suffer death, but after death pass from one body to another". This statement and a few others from classical writers on the same subject has inspired many writers to attempt to prove that Druidism was a deep and venerable philosophy. Despite such attempts, the few early references available that mention the Druids (mainly from a period when they were proscribed and already in decline) show them to have been operators of one of the basic life and death cults common to the western world, and particularly common to the 'Indo-European' races. The folk material handed down to us concerning Druids, from Wales and particularly from Ireland which never came under Roman influence, shows them as priests or magicians of the powers of nature, similar to the Siberian shamans who controlled weather, practiced shape changing, and conversed with the spirits of the dead.

It seems likely, however, that the Druid system was more sophisticated than that of many modern primitive peoples, particularly in the areas of mathematics, law and natural observations linked to religious belief.

In the surviving stories and myths, supported by archaeological evidence, the entrance to the Otherworld is usually a cave, cleft or cavern, a well or spring, a mysterious opening or source of water. In some cases, deep ritual shafts were dug into the ground, from which large amounts of votive offerings have been recovered. The monuments found at Bath surely represent a striking development based upon this concept, showing a period of use from approximately the first to the fourth century A.D. The importance of the springs is only too obvious when we

1. The outlet from the Roman reservoir. The cave-like effect of the arch above the monolithic capstone may well have acquired magical or symbolic value to the Celts and Romans as the cleft that led into the Otherworld....the entry to the hot springs. It was used as an outlet from the reservoir, though this use varied and may not have been constant. The enclosed area retains a powerful and impressive atmosphere to this day, an intuitive insight into the worship of the pagans.

24

consider the large bathing complex itself; but less apparent today is the enclosure and reservoir built specially around the main spring source in the Roman era. This was constructed not only to contain the waters, which are so copious that they caused constant flood problems during the Roman period of occupation of the site, but to give the impression of a steamy vault or cave with a special public access that may have actually led to a platform over the hot waters. An artificial cave has therefore been introduced to replace a natural one, in the same way as deep shafts and votive wells were dug for sacrificial offerings. The cave motif is repeated where the water flows out from the reservoir through the east wall.

This arch (*photograph 1*) may have served as a relieving arch for the lintel immediately below it, and may also have had some symbolic function. It is certain that the side of the culvert and arch triggers a response in modern visitors, arousing some long buried instinct of wonder or mystery....but it is not known whether this was intentional on the part of the buildiers.

Pagan symbolism tended to be spontaneous and the presence of an arch or cave-like orifice attracted magical or unconscious responses particularly when the steaming waters were flowing through as they do today.

A valuable insight into the origin of the site is found within the place name itself....Aquae Sulis. Aquae, of course, is Latin, and means "the waters of", but the term 'Sulis' has never been translated or analysed. In various inscriptions the word Sulis is linked directly to the name Minerva, a Roman goddess, and Sulis is also found in its own right as a separate name specifically referred to as feminine. "To the Goddess Sulis, Lucius Marcus Memor, Haruspex, gave this gift"...."To the Goddess Sulis for the health and safety of Marcus Aufidius Maximus"...."To the Goddess Sulis for the welfare of Gaius Javolenus Saturnalis, imaginifer of the Second Legion Augusta". The Goddess Sulis is mentioned in six dedications from the region of the Temple precinct, and in the memorial of her priest Gaius Calpurnius Receptus found in 1793 in Sydney Gardens across the river from the main site. She is linked with Minerva in an inscription found in the Hot Bath, which has a separate spring, and in another from the Cross Bath which also has its own spring and is thought to have been the focus for another connected religious site. A tenth dedication to Sulis was found in 1861 on the site of the Mineral Water Hospital. The chronicle history of King Bladud, discussed in detail later, states that he set the dedication of his site to "the enchantress Minerva", following the description of Solinus who described the springs and stated that they were presided over by Minerva. Even earlier, the Antonine itinerary, which lists the routes through the Roman provinces of Europe, Asia and Africa, lists the town as "Aquae Sulis".

We can deduce from all this that Minerva and Sulis were goddesses with similar attributes, one being Roman and the other one British or Celtic. Now in both Welsh and old Irish, the word "suil" or "sulis" means an eye, gap or orifice. (The Celtic languages derived from two closely related sources, and it is possible to translate many of the Roman period inscriptions in Britain by comparing them to the earliest versions of the old Celtic tongues that we have available). The natives of the West of England would have spoken a Celtic language, and the term "sulis" is likely to be a native word which describes the nature of the springs and so creates a natural name for the presiding goddess. The place name of Aquae Sulis is therefore a Latin-Celtic joint term which means "The waters of the Gap" or "The waters of the Goddess of the Gap". Names of this sort are very common in Britain and Gaul, both as actual place names and as the names of combined deities. (Similar examples from Britain are: Appollo Cunomaglos....Appollo the runner of the Hounds; Medionemeton....the middle Tree Sanctuary; Loucetio Marti et Nemetona....Mars the lightening god and the goddess of the wood; Aquae Arnemetiae....the waters of the goddess of the grove; Dei Marti Belatucadro....the god Mars, bright and beautiful one. Many other examples are known).

Divine names are almost always functional descriptions, not only of the god or goddess, but of the place of origin. It is sometimes difficult to separate the function and the site of a divine being, as the worship was environmental and each sacred site was thought to be a magical "centre of the world".

The waters of Sul or Sulis, goddess of the gap, would have been particularly important to the Celts for two reasons. The first was that they considered water sources to be extremely sacred, and the second was that they had a religious concept of the creation of life within a boiling cauldron.

Strabo, the geographer, (approx. B.C. 54 — A.D. 21) quotes from the Greek writer Posidonius, who was used as a reference source by many of the classical authors; "as Posidonius and many others have said, the country (i.e. Gaul) being rich in gold, with inhabitants fearing the gods and living frugally, possessed treasures in many parts of the Celtic realm, and the lakes in particular provided inviolability for their treasures, into which they let down heavy masses of gold and silver. The Romans, indeed, when they conquered the region, sold off the lakes by public auction" (Strabo, IV 13). This is confirmed by numerous archaeological sites at wells, springs, and lakes. When Suetonius Paulinus advanced against the Druids at Anglesey, they attempted to stop the Roman soldiers by magical means, and the lake of Llyn Cerrig Bach on the island has yielded an immense hoard of objects from all over Britain. Several writers have suggested that this hoard, which even included chariots, was a desperate last ditch attempt to encourage the Otherworld powers to give aid against the invaders, but it is just as likely to be an accumulation typical to general use and worship.

Offerings of small value have been found in the spring and outlet at Bath, and are described in detail in Cunliffe's "Roman Bath". Any major hoard, however, has long since disappeared, and as the practice referred to by Posidonius describes the Celts before they came under Roman influence, it seems unlikely that there is any hidden treasure to be found today other than the treasures revealed by careful digging and research.

A ritual mask was recovered from the main drain in 1878. (*see photograph 8*). This mask is not only similar to ritual masks from other Roman-Celtic worship sites in Gaul, but is very similar to a modern example found in a folk ritual which has clear and virtually unbroken connections with pagan worship. The Padstow Hobby Horse, which performs a death and resurrection dance on May Day, (the old day of the Celtic Sun God) wears a mask which is surmounted by a tall pointed hat, but the face is comparable to the Bath mask. The Padstow ritual is *genuinely* traditional, handed down through the local families, and is not a revival. Until a few years ago, the ritual itself included a visit to a local pool, with magical actions and associations typical of the Celtic water worship. (The Padstow Hobby Horse is described with various photographs in a very useful book by local author Donald R. Rawe; published Lodenek Press, Padstow, Cornwall).

Lakes, wells and springs were so important to the Celts, that no one would steal the offerings from them....at least until the hard headed Romans came along. The Temple of Delphi also acted as a "bank" in this manner during the height of its long popularity, but it was sacked and plundered several times, including a visit by the Celts in 279 B.C. Obviously the inviolability did not extend to Temples outside the Celtic sphere, though it seems to have been strong enough in the Celtic realms to extend universally despite localised warfare or inter-tribal dispute.

A very detailed analysis of spring and well worship can be found in "Pagan Celtic Britain" by Dr. Anne Ross, who has produced a thorough and complete study of the pagan remains supported by mythical, literary and archaeological references. She says (*page 46*)...."Springs, wells and rivers are of first and enduring importance as a focal point of Celtic cult practice and ritual....the Celtic mother goddesses, who frequently function in the role of war goddesses and prognosticators, have widespread association with water". It is likely that the Romans, who reached Bath in A.D. 43 found a well established worship site, in keeping with the principles outlined that were common to the Celts. There is no direct archaeological evidence that supports this theory, as no major pre-Roman remains have yet been found, but the combination of Celtic Roman terms and images, and the extent of the buildings themselves suggest that the site was one of combined worship and of some importance.

Aquae Sulis can show evidence of Dr. Ross's definitions; of a mother goddess, war goddess, and of foreseeing the future in various forms, in addition to the most obvious feature of therapy, which was associated with the Celtic war goddesses and water powers.

The structure of the Roman reservoir and its enclosure suggest that the spring itself was an object of veneration, and even today many springs and wells in Britain, Ireland and Brittany are still regarded as being magical or effective for certain remedies, though even when their pagan origin is disguised by connection with Christian saints.

If the ritual practices at Aquae Sulis were similar in any way to those at Delphi, or any of the known cave/spring/Otherworld sites, the enclosure would not only have been a viewpoint for the visitor to look at the steaming waters, but might also have been the seat for a seer or seeress inspired by the heady fumes. As we shall discuss later, the British chronicle material associates Bath with necromancy and divination; and there is archaeological support in the form of the dedication of the divinator Lucius Marcus Memor, who gave a statue to the goddess Sulis.

The famous "Bath Curse" shows an interesting negative example of belief in the power of the springs and their attendant goddess...."May he who carried off my Vilbia become as liquid as water. (May) she who obscenely devoured her (become) dumb, whether it is Velvinna, Exsupereus, Verianus, Severinus, Agustalis, Comitianus, Catsuminianus, Germanilla, or Jovina". This curse was recovered in 1880, at the bottom of the reservoir, with the lines inscribed backwards, in typical magical cursing manner.

An inscription of this sort shows a strongly superstitious element rather than a religious one, but is in keeping with the practice of magical cursing that was common in the ancient world. It illustrates the belief that the power of the Otherworld, accessible through spring or cleft presided over by a goddess, was transformable into either positive or negative results, according to the success of the invocation and the manner in which it was carried out. The Celts are known to have sent messages to their ancestors by burning symbols in the fire, thus transporting the essence to the spirit realm, but far more common is the practice of throwing things into water. Even today, the pools and baths are scattered with coins that tourists have dropped in "for luck", so the ancient urge to bargain with the Otherworld is not so far removed from us after all.

Recent excavations have added proof of both the practice of cursing, and that of throwing items of value into the sacred spring. Many additional curses were recovered in 1979, plus a very large number of coins, water-dippers and other artifacts. Future excavations will probably reveal more items of ritual nature, which will be analysed in detail by archaeologists; and it is not the place of the present writer to deal with such finds, other than as supportive evidence for the general patterns of pagan worship suggested at Aquae Sulis.

The Use of Roman God-Names

The prime period of building and development at Bath was during the Flavian era, when there was a deliberate policy of Romanising the subject races. The Romans had emerged from the same fertility and death magic as the less sophisticated peoples that they conquered. Roman worship was derived from Latin and Etruscan roots, fused with powerful Greek influence which permeated a great deal of Roman philosophy, art, and science. The Empire also accepted other cults of eastern origin, and developed a tight system of state controlled Emperor worship for blatantly political reasons. The roots of all worship, however, derived from attempts to relate to the power of the Otherworld, which evolved in time to worship of a mother goddess of life and death with subsequent male consorts or sons, and finally developed into the type of pantheon with which we are familiar from classical sources. The much discussed question of "matriarchy opposed to patriarchy" developed out of examination of this evolution of religion, as various writers claimed that the myths and alterations of the pantheons showed that men were deliberately involved in a take-over from women at quite an early date. Nowadays it is realised that whole question is far more complex and subtle, and that pagan female-power worship was kept up well into the strongly anti-feminist Middle Ages within the core of the male dominated Christian religion.

It was on the level of a mother goddess and a divine son or hero that the Romans were able to relate to the Celtic gods and goddesses, as can be seen at Bath. The highly developed rites and observances of the city of Rome, which spread in various forms through the Empire, were based upon primitive roots, and to make sense of Aquae Sulis we must return again and again to these roots.

One of Bath's world famous exhibits, is the bronze head of Minerva. It was uncovered while digging a sewer, somewhere in Stall Street (which runs through the area of the Temple precinct and springs), though the exact point of its location in uncertain.

This head does not necessarily imply that Minerva in her pure Roman/Greek form was introduced and worshipped from the very beginning of the site at Bath, but does show that she was combined with a native power already present at the source of the hot springs. The joint inscriptions of the period merge her with the goddess Sulis but before developing the symbolic interpretation of Minerva in connection with the hot springs, we must consider how deities were named within the Roman Empire in general, as there is still a great deal of confusion and misunderstanding on the subject.

The identification of gods and goddesses in the ancient world was by no means a rigid or closely structured process. The blending of worship of different powers or differently named gods, such as is found at Bath, was the usual practice, and falls within a definable pattern of relationships between the gods and goddesses which underlies all pagan mythology. The mingling of various dieties was not a liberally generous one on the part of the Roman rulers, but was typical of the general similarities between the various pagan powers, all derived from the common nature worship and magical patterns of relationship to the Otherworld. When Julius Caesar described the gods of the Celts in Gaul, he openly named them by the names of Roman gods. In both classical and post classical writings we find Greek and Roman names freely used when it is perfectly obvious that native deities are being described. This merely provided a set of common reference terms for the educated reader, but it has often led to the misconception that the actual Roman deities in true and historical form are being described. The confusion is further increased by the works of monastic chroniclers and church authorities in the Christian era, who followed the established pattern of the classical authors and Latin Church fathers, describing all pagan gods and goddesses by Latin or Greek names. Fortunately we have numerous exceptions to this rule in inscription, such as the Roman-British dedications described above, and some interesting literary references to the names of non-Roman deities.

To clarify this situation, from which the study of Aquae Sulis seems to have suffered, we need to look at the cultural background, and the political implications of the centralised use of the Greek and Roman pantheons in literary description.

The Roman Empire was made up of numerous races, many religions, and it was not the practice of the rulers to study the language or culture of the conquered 'barbarians'. Government control developed into a system that worked through intermediaries, often hired out through a chain of financial contractors, and enforced by military rule. Local governors and converted tribal leaders were used to the fullest advantage, while geographical or cultural studies were the works of specialists.

When a Roman writer mentions Appollo, or Minerva, or any god or goddess of his own people while he is describing non-Roman worship, he is merely using the names most familiar to him through his own life and experience to describe gods or goddesses *who acted in approximately the same way* as the Roman deities that he lists. There is seldom any suggestion of total identity between the Roman and barbarian worship, and the readers of Caesar, or Tacitus, or any other classical writer Roman or Greek, would have been quite aware that no such suggestion was implied. The names of the gods were functional descriptions. The only exception to this important rule was when exotic cults, such as Mithraism or Christianity, were taken up and kept more or less intact in Roman use and kept their own special god names. After all, there was no need for an educated Roman to refer to the names of conquered peoples' gods....they were in a language unknown to his readers, and would have conveyed nothing!

Pagan deities blended together, merged and changed in a manner that cannot be defined by rigid names. It might seem odd to us to see an altar to Minerva, or a statue of Mars Loucetius in a Christian church, but this is merely due to a long period of domination by one particular religious cult which made a great effort to wipe out all other forms of competition. Exclusion of this sort was quite alien to the Roman mind; and the early Christians were persecuted in Rome *not* for religious reasons, but because their exclusive attitude and consequent refusal to worship the state gods was a subversive political problem. As religion was in no way separate from life or state, those 'persecuted' Christians were in a similar position to a modern terrorist group that refuses to recognise the role of law or government!

The pagan deities formed a pattern of interrelationship, based upon the seasons and the role of Mother and Father powers, and could be broadly related to one central pantheon such as the Greek or Roman. The Celtic gods, however, were particularly slippery, often highly localised, and had a tendency to flow and change their nature according to the cycles of the Moon and Sun within a calculated year. This changing of face can be quite baffling to the modern mind, and even presented the prosaic Romans with some problems which they solved by deliberately Romanising as much as they could under the umbrella of the state. But the Roman writers still used Roman names for the Celtic gods, and these names are clues as to general function and never imply introduction of worship to previously godless barbarians.

Because we find material related to Minerva, Appollo, and Diana at Bath, we should not be so naïve as to think that the Romans imported these images lock stock and barrel, granting them to, or even forcing them upon, the poor benighted natives wallowing in the hot mud. The classical names refer to a combination with Celtic or pre-Celtic deities with similar functions to the Roman images that took them over; but the take-over was by no means absolute, as the name of Sulis and the nature of some of the carvings from the Temple precinct show.

Worship and Magic in Spring and Cave Sites

The principles of worship and magic at Spring and Cave sites were as follows:

1. General worship and propitiation.
2. Education and initiation.
3. Prophecy and divination.
4. Therapy.

Aquae Sulis has evidence of each of these four basic functions, suggesting a significance far beyond that of social bathing with an attendant Temple.

Worship

Worship ranged from actual human sacrifice, banned within the Roman Empire although known to the Romans from their own historical times, through to various rituals both private and public, and the simple engraving of tokens with prayers wishes or curses, dedicated to whatever power was being invoked by the engraver or his customer.

The inscribed stones from Aquae Sulis clearly show the pagan attitude of bargaining with the goddess, where altars are set up in response to the granting of wishes. In this process, the supplicant vows to give a gift to the god or goddess of a sacred site, if only they will grant his specified wish. This is the most superficial proof of the nature of worship, however, and derives from deeper impulses and concepts. Pagan belief should not be judged on this level alone, any more than Christian belief can be judged by the mortuary monuments that clog up the churches and cathedrals. This concept of bargaining is not as naïve as we might think, but stems from the concept of the Otherworld as a dynamic source of energy with which exchanges may be made. The gods and goddesses were beings who were functional aspects of this overall energy, and who might be persuaded to mediate it for mankind, either collectively or individually. Not all divine beings were helpful to mankind, though some specialised in patronage of certain causes or actions or represented the best interests of various natural functions and phenomena.

The gap or gate to the Otherworld was a two-way source, an area of exchange, of constant passing inwards and outwards. This concept occurs again and again in myths and stories about gifts from the gods, and the various vows and commitments always attached to them, or the penalties of misuse. It is further shown by the tales of heroes, aided by a god or goddess, who bring back benefits from the Otherworld for mankind. An important and difficult aspect of this exchange was the human sacrifice, a concept repulsive to the modern reader but happily accepted by his ancestors.

Despite the ban within the Empire, human sacrifice was constantly carried out, and revived at times even within Rome itself by various cults. The human victim was officially replaced by animals, or even offerings of fruit and vegetables. The exterior altar, which stood before the Temple building at Bath, was used for public offerings and rituals and possibly public divinations of a general sort at sacrifices. Such usage replaced the ritual death of humans, intended as an Otherworld exchange and as a method of making spirit links between the outer and inner realms of existence. These sacrificial practices, and the associated cult of the head and head hunting were vital to the Celts, and symbolism derived from head hunting and human sacrifice was retained in Britain well into Christian times, when it finally emerged within the story cycle of the Holy Grail. In an early version of the story, the Grail is a dish holding a severed head.

The carving of a head (known as the "Gorgon's Head" through an error discussed in detail later) on the Temple pediment at Bath exhibits this central function of Celtic belief; though at the time of its carving in the 1st century A.D. it seems unlikely that such ritual killings were carried out at Aquae Sulis. Yet the famous rebellion of Queen Boudicca in A.D. 60 showed a typical reversion to human sacrifice, when the prisoners of this fierce nationalist rebel were impaled on stakes. This was done as an offering to the goddess Andraste, a direct reversion to ritual murder, carried out in a sacred grove, in keeping with Druidic practice as described by the classical authors.

With regard to human sacrifice, the Roman position is a good example of both double standards, and the result of great deal of later colouring and excusing by interpretative writing.

Julius Caesar, for example, made a great deal of the Druids use of human sacrifice (although he may only have been quoting from another source and not referring to personal experience), presumably to strengthen his case for his unnecessary invasion of Gaul (Caesar, The Gallic Wars). Tacitus, who recorded the attack upon the Druid sanctuary at Anglesey, also protested against human sacrifice.

What is seldom realised is that the official use of human sacrifice was well known to the Romans themselves, and was only proscribed officially in the early part of the 1st century B.C. This was virtually contemporary with Caesar, and he would have been familiar with its Roman history as something out of the immediate past; while for Tacitus it was a practice that had ended only a century and a half or so before he recorded the attack on Anglesey (in A.D. 61) and was hardly an institution of the distant past, or something easily forgotten or ignored.

We can assume, perhaps, that the Roman complaints against human sacrifice, which we have from classical literature were therefore political excuses, comparing a new outlook with an old one, and showing civilisation as opposed to barbarism.

The overall impression of the Romans' attitude towards the human sacrifice is twofold; firstly, the suppression of the human sacrifice was closely tied with the strengthening of state controlled worship, for human sacrifice was usually associated with inspirational matters from the Otherworld, guidance by ancestral spirits, and similar difficult elements which were not easy to control or to direct or suppress. Secondly, and more subtly, human sacrifice for *religious* purposes was not *urbane*, it was the hallmark of the barbarian. Continual ritualistic slaying in the Circus was allowable *for entertainment*, however, and this was civilisation! The entire question was not one of morality at all, but of viability of cultural behaviour. No doubt the Romans would consider many of the practices of *our* civilisation as horribly uncouth and savage, even though we have abolished the death penalty in Britain, and seldom kill people "just for fun".

The usual animal of sacrifice was the bull or ox, the standard symbolic powerful victim of the ancients. Numerous other beasts were also used, and fowls were killed for augury. The Celts were still sacrificing bulls in Scotland and Ireland as late as the 18th or even 19th centuries, as we know from various folk customs and the lamentations and unheeded prohibitions of the worthy clergymen of various Christian sects. Animal sacrifice often involved a subsequent communal meal, a type of ritual often elaborated upon in secret as well as held in public. In the cults of Mithras and Jesus, bread and wine were substituted for the blood and body of the bull or man, but were supposed to change magically into the real thing at the peak of the ritual.

General worship merges imperceptibly with the other functions of any religious site, as all magical acts depend upon the assumption that it is possible to gain benefit from Otherworld sources. Many dedicated items can be seen in the Museum next to the Great Bath, ranging from the famous collection of gemstones (analysed by M. Henig in "Roman Bath") to the bronze head of Minerva. The Temple and associated buildings are obvious evidence of worship in themselves, as are the dedicatory inscriptions.

Education & Initiation

Education and initiation techniques were extremely important within the pagan worship, which was far more dependant upon actual practice of ritual than upon faith or dogma. The main objective was to teach and develop an ability to work in harmony with whatever divine power was involved. Education took the form of methods for coping with life after physical death, and instruction into the secrets thought to be locked in Nature. These methods were taught by myth and by practical demonstration. Public rituals were often the outer forms of more esoteric magical practices, in which the initiate was given individual training in matters not available to all. The training undertaken by the Druids was supposed to last twenty years, and involved formidable tasks of memory and self control. Druidic knowledge was unwritten, and committed to memory, although the Druids did have knowledge of writing. This oral dependence is common to all early cultures, a good example being the body of Roman law, which was retained by memory and popular use well into the period of literacy. Many of the old oral teachings, once regarded as religious or magical, passed into folk tradition and were written down in various forms by the monastic chroniclers, while some survived into the present century where they still exist as popular superstition.

The initiatory aspects of the old religions, particularly those concerned with the

34

forces of nature, passed on into the Christian era, merged with the influx of Arabic influence in the Middle Ages, and finally flowered as the art of alchemy from which all modern physics and chemistry has evolved. The emphasis within alchemy was that the operator had to be pure in soul, and alter his very awareness, to carry out a successful physical experiment. This is nothing more than refined echo of the primitive shaman, Druid, or seer, who penetrated into the spirit world through fasting, trance and ritual.

It is amusing to note that Bath was particularly attractive to alchemists, because of its seething mineral waters. One churchman was severely censured for his alchemical interests, and only allowed to keep his position in the Abbey if he gave them up and refunded the church money spent on his research.

The pagan intuitions about the origins of life were often symbolised by a seething cauldron, a symbol taken up by the alchemists with their special sealed crystal vessels, and obviously visible in simplistic terms in the actual physical site of the Hot Springs themselves. The educational and initiatory processes of the pagans were also concerned with therapy....but the last trace of this has now disappeared from Bath, with the current medical opinion that the hot mineral waters are of no value in treatment, despite the long tradition of healing and the numerous hospital buildings with attested cures, now closed down.

Prophecy

Prophecy was reckoned to be one of the most tangible results and benefits of the operation of the two previous functions of worship and initiation. Prophecy was generally carried out by specialists who were trained for the job, though it could occur as an inspiration or possession during the more excitable public rituals. Prophecy was based upon the belief that the divine powers controlled the flow of energies from the Otherworld and could give information, instruction and actual pre-vision of what was going to happen next. The human sacrifice was closely linked to the prophetic function, as the spirits of the dead and the ancestors that had passed into the Otherworld were supposed to communicate to the seer or seeress whatever was asked of them. Early primitive people actually lived with the skulls and bones of their ancestors within their dwellings, while the more urbane Romans kept busts of their illustrious forebears....simply an evolution of the same concept. The practice was kept up by the Christians, of course, in their worship of scraps of bone, rag, wood, skulls, and other relics, as a means of linking with the Saints in Heaven who seem suspiciously like the Ancestors in a different disguise.

One of the most interesting inscriptions left to us reads "To the Goddess Sulis, Lucius Marcius Memor, haruspex, gave this gift". A haruspex was a member of a specific order of soothsayers who foretold the future by the observation of animal entrails, the circumstances of the sacrifice, or by the direction of the fire or its smoke. They were adopted by the Romans from the Etruscans, and their original methods were connected with the human sacrifice. In Roman tradition they were said to have been introduced to the city by the hero Romulus. This order of augerers was in operation throughout Roman history until the reign of the Emperor

Constantine, who became a Christian and banned all soothsaying on pain of death. The presence of a haruspex lends further weight to the importance of the site of Aquae Sulis, though we have no way of knowing if he was a visitor or a resident priest who worked in the Temple. He may well have been following the common practice of visiting distant oracles in search of replies to specific questions. His statue gift, of which only the base remains, would have been in response to a specific prophecy or gift of healing. If we could have recovered the statue itself, it would have given us a further clue to his reasons for being in Aquae Sulis, as gifts often reflected the intentions of the giver in the symbolic form of gods, goddesses, or animals.

The overall interpretation of the site of Aquae Sulis has never been clearly established. Cunliffe states...."23 acres, much of it occupied by monumental buildings, is hardly an adequate area for a town of normal type, nor is there any evidence to suggest that Bath ever served as a seat of local government, but a glance at the map emphasises very strongly Bath's important position as a market centre....it is in no way unusual for a great religious site to become a market centre, and there are many similar examples in the Roman world".

Bath could well have been the main prophetic centre for a group of worship sites in the West of England, all of which show similar elements of therapy, water, and related deities. The famous Temple of Nodens at Lydney would have been similar in its cult use to Bath, and a loosely defined area from Bath to the Cotswolds and over into the Severn area of Wales exhibits broad cultural similarities. If Aquae Sulis was already a centre of a death and Otherworld cult, operating prophetic and therapeutic services when the Romans took it over, it would have been under Druid influence, but by the first century A.D. the Druid priests or priestesses would have been replaced, possibly by the haruspices. It is interesting to remember that the Boudiccan rebellion and the Roman destruction of the Druid sanctuary at Anglesey were within one year of each other, at exactly the time when archaeologists suggest the Roman buildings at Bath were under way. The Priest of the Goddess Sulis, Gaius Calpurnius Receptus, lived to the ripe old age of 75, as we know from his memorial altar which was found in nearby Sydney Gardens in 1793. So in addition to possible haruspices, there were priests who probably practiced an amalgamated Roman-British type of worship.

Therapy

The curing of diseases was thought to be possible by the divine energies of the healing god or goddess invoked, and was also aided by direct physical treatment. Bathing, mud and heat treatments, and the use of herbs, were very common in a combination of observed and proven medicine and sympathetic magic. Some sites are known from classical descriptions to have practiced a type of psychotherapy. This was a ritualised dream therapy, often in the form of an image or images connected with the deity of the site. This magical dreaming was greatly favoured by the Celts, who employed specific dream rituals which feature in various early tales and myths and survived as folk custom for many centuries. Psychotherapy is a

36

modern restatement of the combined forces of worship and practical magic, ritualising the subject's problems and externalising them for understanding.

Bath has such a long history of therapy, which is so well documented, that it is not necessary to repeat it here. It ranges from the story of the curing of King Bladud's scabby pigs, through centuries of treatment for rheumatism and other diseases. The entire concept of therapy in the pagan world was inseperable from that of fertility, the flow of power that balanced life and death. It was for this reason that so many of the early goddesses were related to war and therapy, life and death, and also to the flow of waters symbolically emerging from the underworld or Otherworld.

We are now able to examine the goddess Sulis, or Sulis Minerva, in the light of her context as a Celtic and Roman deity.

The Goddess

The Goddess

To build up a picture of the Goddess Sulis Minerva we must refer to our several sources; archaeology, classical literature, and the native written and oral traditions which are pertinent to Bath. The word Sulis (or Suilis) as previously stated, means an eye, gap or orifice. This is directly relevant to the nature of the site itself, where hot water emerges from gaps within the ground, from the bedrock of liassic clay. There are, in fact, several connected spring sources, the main one being famous for supplying about quarter of a million gallons of hot water daily.

We know that 'Sulis' was the name of the local goddess, from her inscriptions, and that she was linked to the Roman Minerva. The only reference to the goddess Sulis is at Bath, but this is not surprising, as Celtic or British deities often had a strictly local identity relating to the environment. The overall attributes of the gods and goddesses, however, show clearly recognisable patterns, so we can identify Sulis by the following means:
1. She was a goddess of hot springs.
2. She includes in her name the meaning "orifice or gap".
3. She was responsible for therapy.

These basic attributes are defined by the inscriptions, the geology, and the native language, and it is possible to suggest further elements of her nature by comparing her to similar native goddesses. The Celtic goddesses of springs were powers of fertility and therapy, also war goddesses, with an additional connection with prophecy. These functions were related, as we have seen, through the concept of the Otherworld, source of life and death energy, the key to the future. There is no reason to assume that Sulis, with the three basic attributes that we have, was any different from other aspects of this type of goddess....and there is plenty of additional evidence to support the theory that she was, indeed, a pre-Roman deity similar to the fierce and powerful beings that we know of from Irish, Welsh, and other native traditions dating back to magical and mythical originals.

Sulis may be further revealed by her link and amalgamation with Minerva, who was not only a Roman addition to the native goddess, but had strong connections with another widespread Celtic goddess whom the Romans naturally described by the name 'Minerva'. We have additional dedications to the Suleviae, (a term of respect used for the group of Mother Goddesses) and Diana (Originally a Latin goddess of the hunt, but with far reaching symbolic connections which link her to sites such as Bath).

Minerva is clearly the major goddess linked to the site in the Roman and post-Roman periods, as so much evidence shows, but Sulis still maintained her own dedications and priesthood, so it is not possible to suggest that she died out or was in any way suppressed. Indeed, the very dedications that we might expect to be given to Minerva, such as that of the haruspex, were given to Sulis, and despite the limited evidence in inscription, it seems certain that the native goddess retained a strong personal identity by which she was known abroad, and by which she attracted visitors.

2. A very primitive representation of the "Three Mothers" or Triple Goddess, shown in the museum at Bath, although not directly from the site of the springs.

Minerva is a highly developed combination of various goddesses, and like most pagan powers she accumulated connections and attributes through her long history of cultural development and exchange, without ever totally hiding her primitive roots. She is partly derived from a Roman adaptation of the Greek goddess Athena, and in the broadest sense she was worshipped as one who protected and guided the growth of human culture and evolution. The ancient goddesses were often said to be triplicate in appearance and nature (*see photograph 2 for a very primitive plaque from the Bath area that illustrates this*), three phases of one power. The first was a maiden, virgin or young woman, the second a fruitful mother, and the third an old crone. The origin of this triplication is very simple, and provides a useful key to any consideration of the goddesses and their seemingly complex interrelationships; the first shows youthfulness, purity and a spirit of beginning or initiation; the second shows fruitfulness and maturity, a spirit of achievement; while the third shows decline, breakdown and death, a spirit of natural conclusion. The goddesses were worshipped separately and collectively, but inevitably lead into one another in a ceaseless cycle of birth-life-death-and ultimately rebirth.

Minerva belongs to the first aspect....for she was a virgin goddess, and concerned with helping mankind. She is credited with numerous gifts, such as the invention of numbers, wind instruments, and the protection of both artists and warriors. By extension she became the goddess of clear thinking, wisdom and good health, both mental and physical. Her protection of peaceful and warlike pursuits may seem odd at first, but as the goddess she was the source and reconcilier of opposites. She naturally held the forces that govern human development within her grasp, and these forces are both positive and negative. Her special favourites were heroes, she is the patroness of several in mythology, to whom she gave gifts, advice, and actual help when necessary. This process shows how the pagans symbolised the drives of development and evolution within culture....it was the hero who *acted* but it was the goddess who *granted* the gifts and the opportunities to use them. In time some of these heroes became gods in their own right. Minerva was said to have sprung fully armed from the head of her father Zeus, and in this we can detect an echo of her more primitive origins. She is a development of goddesses such as the Celtic "Morrigan"...."The Morrigan was one of a trio of war goddesses who appear in Irish tradition, influencing the outcome of battle by magic and by inspiring terror into the hearts of warriors. Possessing marked sexual characteristics, and appearing frequently in ornithomorphic or animal guise, this powerful group of goddesses reveals convincingly all the qualities and attributes suggested by the iconography and epigraphy. Appearing at one moment as terror inspiring hags, at the next as beautiful young women, and yet again as beaked crows or ravens, these goddesses figure with impressive frequency throughout the earliest stratum of Irish mythological tradition. Their names vary, Morrigan seemingly being a collective term for the group as well as being one of the individual goddesses". This extract from Dr. Ross's "Pagan Celtic Britain" summarises the changing behaviour of pagan goddesses in general, but by the time of the 1st century A.D. the Roman and Greek conceptions had generally separated the triple functions.

The amalgamation of Sulis with Minerva is understandable when we consider that they each had common primitive origins; and even more obvious when we see that as a bringer of civilisation and control, Minerva was an essential cultural replacement for the fierce goddesses such as Andraste or the Morrigan, with their wild unpredictability and insistance on human sacrifice. Despite her fully armed beginning, Minerva had grown into a more peaceful figure by the time she came to Bath, a symbol of Roman style common-sense and discipline ruling over the wilder side of elemental nature. Julius Caesar, either copying from Posidonius or speaking from his own observations, includes "Minerva" as one of the main goddesses of the Celts....by which he means a goddess of similar attributes. The goddess who fits this description very well is Brigit, or Brigantia, tribal deity of the Brigantes, but also widespread among the Celts in general, and revered for centuries as St. Brigit in Scotland and Ireland. Minerva is clearly equated with Brigantia on a classical style relief from Birrens in Yorkshire, where she is also linked to Victory.

In Cormac's "Glossary", dating from about 900 A.D., Brigit or Brighid is linked to poetry, learning, divination and prophecy. Saint Brigit is connected with several "holy wells", and with therapy; and has many other blatantly fire-and-light-keeping pagan attributes, such as hanging her cloak on the beams of the Sun, bringing the first light of Spring (from Scots folk custom) and being in charge of fire itself. The 12th century historian, ecclesiastic and diarist Gerald of Wales (Giraldus Cambrensis) tells us that St. Brigit and her nuns guarded a perpetual fire, which links her immediately to Minerva. Solinus, describing Bath in the 3rd century, mentions a similar sacred eternal flame or fire. The entire story is taken up again by Geoffrey of Monmouth, and the "eternal flame" was an important aspect of pagan temples, a symbol of the undying sun or light that triumphed over the darkness of winter and death. It has been suggested that the ashes of a coal fire, discovered during excavations of the Temple at Bath, are the remains of the Eternal Fire itself.

The picture of Sulis-Minerva is therefore one of a goddess who mediates the powers of the Otherworld in a manner that is beneficial to mankind; she teaches the arts and sciences of peace and war, brings healing, and controls the eternal fire or energy of the Sun. Minerva was often called Belisama, a name that means "exalted or bright one", and the very names of Brigit, Bride, or Briggidda, relate to our modern word 'bright'.

The steaming waters of Aquae Sulis would have been thought of as heated by the eternal fire, which renewed the vigour of the Sun in Winter, and the actual fire kept burning within the Temple was a visible sign of this energy. The motif of the Sun travelling to the Otherworld to be reborn is a common one in numerous solar myths, either on a seasonal or on a daily basis. One of the prime symbols of the Otherworld was the cauldron, a vessel of immortality. A native Welsh goddess, Keridwen, of ferocious aspect like the Morrigan, was the brewer of a cauldron of all knowledge. In varying forms, the cauldron occurs again and again in folk tales and myths, as the vessel of the Otherworld. In the Welsh story of "Branwen, daughter of Llyr", a magical cauldron features...."I will add even more to your compensation", said Bran"for I will give you a cauldron, the property of which is this; take a man who has been slain today and throw him into it, and tomorrow he will fight as well as ever, only he will not be able to speak" (from the Mabinogion, trans. Jeffrey Gantz). Yet another Celtic tale describes a pot into which pigs leapt to be cooked, and after they were eaten, all that had to be done was to throw the bones back in, and they were restored to wholeness. The physical site of the hot springs would have been an obvious locality for such a cauldron of immortality, so it is not surprising that the goddess Sulis-Minerva with her various fire keeping and guardian and therapeutic powers was the presiding deity. The pagans saw the environment as being wholly related to their understanding of divine powers, there was no intellectual separation such as has developed in the intervening centuries, and although we discuss the remains in terms of 'symbolism', it seems very likely that sites such as Delphi, or Bath, or any of the other non-political nature-based sites, were considered to be *in reality* the gates to the Otherworld. The advent of state control of the 'political' religions, which culminated in the total state cult of Roman Christianity, shows the growth of intellectual separation from religion, and the increasing awareness of its usefulness as a tool of suppression. There is often a difficulty in examining the pre-state or pre-Christian cults, which is the direct result of conditioning and education derived from a religious programme that is quite alien to their outlook.

The eternal fire at Bath was said never to have died down, but to have been perpetually re-lit from rocky lumps. A similar fire at Kildare in Ireland was kept burning well into the Christian era, when it was put out by the invading English. The eternal temple flame was probably the origin of the alchemical "eternal lamps" which were supposed to burn forever without need of refuelling. In Rome, the sacred fire was associated with the famous Vestal Virgins....the goddess Vesta being similar in some ways to Minerva, but without the primitive warlike connections. Her eternal fire was supposed to have been brought by Aeneas from the sacked city of Troy, a theme that we shall see recurring in the myth history of Britain and its reference to the native founder of Bath, King Bladud.

The additional inscription to Diana comes from the Hot Bath. "To the most hallowed Goddess Diana, Vettius Benignus, a freedman, fulfilled his vow". Diana is not at all out of context at Aquae Sulis. She was the primitive hunting goddess of the Latins, a virgin-huntress, and the director of the Moon. She sometimes rode a chariot drawn by stags, and was associated with the boar hunt. She was a goddess who brought death, and could cause pestilence with her arrows, exactly like her solar brother Appollo. As the Greek goddess Artemis, she was shown in triple form, her fruitful aspect being represented by a figure with many breasts, and her fearful aspect merging with the ancient goddess of the Underworld, Hecate. She also guarded women in childbirth, and controlled the deaths of elderly females in order to renew life with the birth of young girls. Perhaps Vettius' vow was in connection with a successful childbirth.

The 'Luna Pediment' (*see photograph 3*) is a relief of a goddess backed by a full and crescent Moon, bearing a whip, with her hair tied up in the form of a shell. She is a ruler of water, and of the female mysteries. There is no reason to assume that this is strictly 'Luna', for it could be the 'Diana' referred to by Vettius Benignus, and could, in fact, be the goddess Sulis.

3. The goddess Luna. Shown in head and shoulders relief, she is supported by a device which shows both full and crescent moons, and horns, as one symbolic disc. Her hair is tied up to represent sea-shells, showing her rule over the tides, and she carries a staff and thong, or whip, as an emblem of power and control. This implement may represent her rule over horses, which would integrate this image with the widespread Celtic goddess of horses, who was one of the major native deities. Cunliffe

44

suggests that this image would have fitted over the facade of the Four Seasons, which he proposes for reasons of architectural harmony. Curiously, the Celts reckoned their seasons by lunar and not solar calculations, so the structural possibility of such a placement of the Luna pediment may have some symbolic background that bridges classical and native use, as is very plain with the solar pediment that fronted the Temple of Sulis Minerva.

45

If the image is meant to be Sulis, she makes a balanced image to fit with the solar figure on the main Temple pediment (*discussed in the chapter on the "Gorgon's Head"*). Professor Cunliffe suggests that this image could have been part of the "Facade of the Four Seasons", for reasons of architectural balance, and that the Facade may have been situated at the entrance to the enclosure of the sacred spring. A further strengthening of both of these possibilities, is that they would fit with the overall structure of symbolism developed in temple patterns and images, where the deities were often paired and male and female cult Temples were separate, but closely connected.

Her possible placing on the Facade of the Four Seasons raises an interesting question, of some importance in identifying the Goddess herself. Is it a representation of the Seasons....or is it something else? So much of the structure is missing that no firm definition can be made, and the seasonal reading as shown by Cunliffe, and the earlier interpreters Lysons, Irvine and Haverfield, is by far the most likely, fitting well with the conceptual pattern of the pagan seasonal worship. But an additional reading can be added to this seasonal base, for it was usually expressed as an adventure or myth, such as that of Perseus who was patronised by Minerva (*discussed in the section on the "Gorgon's Head"*). Bearing in mind the fact that the patron goddess is closely identified with the aiding of solar-heroes, either as a Celtic or Roman power, the Facade may additionally have shown such a myth, presided over by the Goddess who controls the flow of the Seasons (the Celtic seasons were assessed, by lunar and not by solar calculations), and also the fate of the characters within the myth. One clue to the amplification of this theme is the "Cupid" holding a sickle. Although these figures are usually supposed to signify seasonal activities, they could equally well show the phases of the myth, for the sickle was the implement of death and winter, by which the virile young god overcame the sterile old god, and which the hero used to slay monsters. Perhaps the large missing figures will be found during future excavation.

The Gorgon's Head

In 1790, the main blocks of a carved pediment were discovered. It is accepted that these blocks were found more or less where they fell or were thrown, as they are of massive size, and that they are on the site of their original building. This turned out to be the classical style Temple, nowadays called 'The Temple of Sulis Minerva'. The carved blocks are exhibited in the Museum on the site, and a rather poor restoration can be seen in nearby Sydney gardens, built as a park shelter or summer house. (*see photograph 7*).

The pediment features a powerful male head, with various supporting symbolic carvings of figures and other related elements. The head is seen in full face, as a deep relief carving, and is typical of the Celtic male as decribed by classical writers. "Their aspect is terrifying, they are very tall in stature with rippling muscles....they look like wood demons, their hair thick and shaggy like a horses mane....some leave a moustache that covers the whole mouth and when they eat and drink it acts like a sieve, trapping particles of food....". This account, written in the 1st century A.D. by Diodorus Siculus, is a typical classical description of the Celts, and it fits the glowering hairy image at Bath quite well. But the head itself goes far beyond this simple identity, for the hair and moustaches are stylised into waving flames, in which can be seen a pair of wings, and large prominent ears. (*see photograph 4*). The head is not, therefore, a naturalistic representation, although it is strongly life-like and vivid, but is a symbolic one. The head was a vital religious object to the Celts, and as this Bath head combines both native and classical attributes, it is surely an image of importance in our interpretation of the site as a whole.

Until a few years ago, before the reorganisation of the museum, the head was labelled "an unusual male Medusa" and has perpetually been referred to by archaeologists as the "Gorgon's Head", even when it is obvious that something more is involved. The error arose through the mental attitude of the early researchers and archaeologists who first worked on the site, for they had had a "classical" education; they generally related all finds to the Greek and Roman pantheon and myths, and tended to pass over Celtic material as being too uncertain. In recent years, however, a great deal has been learned about the early people of Europe, and we have far more information available to us from archaeology, fresh translations of literature and reinterpretations of cultural patterns, than the pioneer archaeologists could have imagined. Without the pioneers, of course, we might not have any of it at all! As early as the middle of the 19th century there were writers who recognised the true identity of the carved head; but they were in the minority, and suffered from the general reluctance to give any credit to native material unless it was absolutely unavoidable.

The head contains many non-classical features....in fact is hardly classical in concept at all, being a Celtic image in the midst of classical supporters, sticking out quite blatantly. The labelling of the head 'an unusual male Medusa' gives the impression that it was a freak, a rare departure from an accepted norm, yet this is not true, for the head can be proved to be in the mainstream of native symbolism,

4. *The stylised head of the Celtic Sun God, Belinus or Bel, identified by the Greeks and Romans with Appollo. His waving flaming hair discloses his wings and ears, typical solar attributes for an all-seeing all-hearing god. Although the head is constructed in such a way as to be a full face in flattened relief, similar to metalwork of the period, the presence of two intertwined snakes around the lower part may suggest a torque, the Celtic neck ornament of magical power, which symbolised the union with the forces of nature. This head is likely to be that of the being referred to by Geoffrey of Monmouth as "King Bladud", a master of magic and necromancy in the Druid tradition.*

therefore quite normal and in keeping with an amalgamated Roman-Celtic worship site. Heads abound in Celtic archaeological remains, although the Bath head is a particularly fine example of both craftsmanship and character. A full discussion of its possible origins, and the overall style and dimension of the whole pediment is published in the Journal of Roman studies, 1955, but the opinion of the authors, Richmond and Toynbee, as to the nature of the god himself, seems quite at variance with our knowledge of native worship, and even with the actual details of the carving itself. They see it as a water deity wreathed with leaves and snakes, whereas it is more likely to be a sun god, and can in fact be identified as such from various sources of evidence. The whole question is fraught with interpretative problems, many of which can be resolved by application to the old traditions relating to Bath itself. In fact, there should be no conflict between a classical 'gorgon' interpretation, if it is correctly expressed, and a more Celtic or native 'sun-head' reading, for both were known at the time of building, and the end result that we see today must surely have satisfied all comers.

One of the earliest, and most thorough examinations of the Head, was that made by the Rev. Professor Sayce, MA,LLD, in 1890. (His analysis of the subject was read to the 'Honourable Society of Cymmrodorion', and appears in their journal 'Y Cymmrodor', vol X, pp207-221, 1890).

Although this study had been listed by Levis, in his book 'The British King who tried to Fly', it has virtually been ignored in all archaeological literature referring to the site; but it still has valid points to offer, even if they are dated and superceded by modern standards. Despite the fact that Professor Sayce seems to have been the earliest writer to call the goddess 'Sul', and not 'Sulis', he at least differentiates between the goddess and the god, and continues to offer proof of the solar identity of the carved Head, and that it is surely 'King Bladud'.

Referring to the head itself he says "It bears a close resemblance to the head of the Phoenician sun-god carved in similar fashion on the platform of the Romano-Phoenician temple at Rakleh, on Mount Hermon, by the side of the figure of the eagle, the Emblem of Zeus. In Assyrian mythology, the eagle was the emblem of 'the midday sun'."

Sayce also raises the interesting discussion as to *who* was actually worshipped in the Temple.

"But the flaming face of which I have spoken proves that there was such a god by the side of the goddess, and it further shows that while the goddess was worshipped in a separate temple, the hot springs themselves and the baths that stood above them were under the protection of the god. The baths, in fact, were his temple. He must, therefore, have been the god of the hot springs, the heat of which would explain his identification with the solar orb. The burning heat of the springs and of the sun were imagined to proceed from the same source. The god of the springs was a form of sun god, but of that sun god of the nether world, for whom, as Professor Rhys has shown, the Kelts had a special predilection".

In fact, the Temple Pediment has been taken for granted as that of Sulis-Minerva, but it could equally well be that of the sun god himself, as he is the major figure dominating its entrance. The goddess is more likely to have presided over the spring enclosure described by Cunliffe, while the baths themselves were used for therapeutic and religious practices associated with the overall cult. A pattern of this sort would be very much in keeping with general pagan symbolism, and with classical usage in particular.

The head is also referred to as 'a British Sun god', with a photograph, by the writer Lewis Spence, in his study of 'The Magic Arts in Celtic Britain', published in 1946.

Richmond and Toynbee state: "The 'Gorgon' states in the clearest possible terms that these pedimental sculptures were the work of a Celtic artist, trained in a classical school, but transposing the themes that he had learnt there into the native idiom of his race. Part of that idiom is the subtle blending in the mask of snakes, locks and wings — so subtle that it is by no means easy, at first glance, to pick out the six uncrested heads of the female snakes. And it takes some thought to disentangle the two crested males, which are knotted together below the 'gorgon's' chin".

The general interpretation that they offer is that the god is a symbol of the water-power of the springs, exactly as Sayce suggested; but whereas he saw the god as being solar, Richmond and Toynbee see it as being primarily a water deity.

Dr. Ross says "Heads are portrayed on other reliefs from Roman Britain. Several of these bear a resemblance to the classical Gorgon or Medusa heads. This type, although having no obvious religious significance in classical times, shows traces of a long ancestry among the Indo-Euorpeans, where in all probability it originated as a solar symbol. Later under classical influence, it became crystallised as a staring, serpent wreathed symbol of evil-averting power. Placed on temple porticos, eaves of buildings, and shields in the same contexts as those in which the Celtic "tête coupée (severed head) was exhibited, the symbol of the Gorgon head shared with the Celtic heads in apotropaic powers, but had lost the divine association of the Celtic heads....deeply indigenous cults could thus be masked under the image of Medusa, only the individuality of expression, the vigour of execution and the male sex of the heads betraying their non classical origin...." She continues by comparing the Bath head to those of Chester and Caerleon, carved in similar style. The Caerleon head has serpents in the beard, as does the Bath one, but none of these heads seem to be Gorgons proper, as Dr. Ross takes great care to explain. As two distinct streams of symbolism have merged or become confused in interpretation here, it is interesting to consider each of them, and then realise how they blended together at Aquae Sulis.

Medusa

Medusa was a Gorgon, one of three sisters who are typical examples of the primitive triplication already referred to. In her original form, Medusa was the young maiden of the three, but in time they all acquired the hideous aspects for which they are famous. They were able to turn all who looked upon them to stone, a very important prohibition or taboo which is found in nature and fertility worship on all levels, from the most basic and primitive, to the highly developed phases such as the classical myth that we are examining. Certain places, or more specifically, certain times of the year or phases of the Moon, were hedged around with secrets linked to the cycles of fertility. It is often stated in studies of early religions, or even of classical myths, that the people who produced them were not aware of the role of the male in reproduction. This hardly fits with the obvious knowledge of the female fertility cycle that myths and taboos show us, for if knowledge of the male contribution to conception was lacking, there was hardly any need for the numerous restrictions which eventually evolved into the Gorgon mask hiding Temple secrets in the pagan tradition. The taboos, of course, were never intended as a condemnation of womanhood....but a little common sense suggests that their origin was to ensure that maximum opportunities for conception were guaranteed, as the non-fertile period of the month was under a magical prohibition from the goddess, or later, the god.

Another more abstract interpretation of the Gorgon as an apotropaic or guardian mask, is that no one may look directly upon the face of nature, or the true secrets of life. For this reason, the ancient goddesses, such as Isis, were shown veiled. The reasoning behind this concept still holds good today, for life is seen from the viewpoint of one's own limitations, and to suddenly penetrate beyond them is to risk madness....an occurrence found in several ancient myths.

The classical writers Hesiod and Appollodorus both state that Medusa was given her hideous appearance and serpent-hair as the result of a curse by Minerva/ Athena. Athena, being a virgin goddess, was extremely offended to find Medusa making love with Poseidon the sea god, in her very own Temple. This was the most blatant of sacrileges and insults. As Medusa had long and beautiful hair, Athena changed it into serpents as part of her curse. After this transformation, the now malignant Medusa was an anti-human supernatural being, and as such was hunted and destroyed by the hero Perseus, who is typical of a long line of such saviours, heroes and kings, all broadly associated with the symbolism of the Sun.

Perseus flew with the help of winged shoes and helmet, given to him by Pluto, which made him invisible. He was given a magical mirror by Athena, in which he could look at the Gorgon without being turned to stone, and a scythe by Hermes to cut off her head. Athena eventually placed the severed head on her shield, where it retained its magical power. The Gorgon's head was used to guard Temples and other buildings and their secrets, from human and non-human spies.

The ramifications of this myth are numerous. Medusa, originally part of a primitive trinity, was changed from beauty to excessive ugliness, through the weakness of her unrestrained passion. Athena, who made the change, was a virgin goddess, patroness of the solar hero who represents mankind conquering the ancient fear of Nature. When the conquest was made, the trophy of the head was used to guard those same secrets that it had abused. There is a worn carving of

Minerva from the site at Bath, in which a faint head can be seen, radiating snaky locks, or sunrays, on the goddess' breast. (*see photograph 5*). The entire tale, in which Perseus is gifted by various gods, is typical of a solar passage through the year, but it also attempts to show the evolution of human awareness out of group fear into individual development and enlightenment. Minerva/Athena was specifically the patroness of this process, and the whole tale was brought about by her own magic in the first place!

When early archaeologists found a guardian head, related to the Temple site, they conveniently labelled it as a "Gorgon", but the reader will have realised from the story and from the photograph of the actual carving itself, that what was discovered in 1790 was more "Perseus" than "Medusa".

The knot has a few more twists to it yet! The unchallenged assumption that the Bath head is actually Medusa, albiet sex-changed, has led to various diagrams and copies showing the head wreathed in snakes, which replace the clearly visible wings and flames. There *are*, however, snakes to be seen around the lower part of the face, coiling together and emerging to the right and left of the cheeks. They look very much like the snake headed terminals of a neck torque, the Celtic ornament of magical potency associated with fertility and solar gods. Can it be that our "Medusa" is really a native god?

The Magical Head

The early Celts were head hunters. "In exactly the same way as hunters do with the skulls of the animals that they have slain....(the Celts), preserved the heads of their most high ranking victims in cedar oil, keeping them carefully in wooden boxes". So says Diodorus, and his statement is confirmed by archaeological evidence. Temples, such as the famous sanctuary at Roquepertuse in France which would have been in the Celtic realm, had niches for skulls or preserved heads. In British remains from the Roman period, there are a very large number of magical or religious head carvings of obvious native origin. One of the most interesting features of the Bath head, as Richmond and Toynbee show in their article, is that the style of *carving* is influenced by classical training, but the *image itself* is entirely Celtic. The very Capitol of Rome was traditionally the site of a bleeding head, severed and set in place as a magical guardian. The motif is expressed in the British myth of Bran, King of all Britain, which clearly indicates the primitive head worship known through both Celtic and Roman traditions. The sacred head was such a strong concept that it passed into the Christian tradition, where the magical skulls found at pagan wells were suddenly re-named as Saints. The tomb of Saint Cuthbert at Durham contained a severed head, which is significant as he was an advocate of the old style Celtic Christianity at the synod of Whitby in 664 A.D. After the synod Roman papal Christianity gradually took over, and the native influenced version was suppressed. We shall see a further reference to this change of religion in the myth of King Bladud, discussed in the next chapter.

The Head as a magical trophy or centre of power can be traced to a group of important tales, myths and poems, in which a hero invades the Otherworld, and

5. A native carving of the goddess Minerva. A faint head can be seen upon her breast, which radiates lines. Is this the Gorgon's head that turned all who gazed upon it to stone?

brings back marvellous gifts for the benefit of his people. In this, we can see a similarity to the pursuit of the Gorgon by Perseus. One of the best known examples of the Severed Head as a magical token comes from a collection of early Welsh stories known as "The Mabinogion". The first manuscript source of these fascinating and highly entertaining tales is in the White Book of Rhydderch, c. 1325. This late date of the collection of the tales under one cover does not apply to the age of the contents. They have clear connections with early pagan themes, and are essentially pre-Christian. They compare well to classical sources that describe the Celts, and with the Irish myths and folk tales. The story of Bran runs through the tale "Branwen, daughter of Llyr", and is also found in a curious old Welsh poem, "The Spoils of Annwyn". The first story mentions the magical cauldron, while the poem describes an attempt to plunder such a device from the Otherworld. The poem is so peculiar and formalised, that many translators have suggested that it is a relic of an actual ritual verse; but the basic content is that a raid was made, wonders and terrors were endured, and only a few returned.... transformed by their adventure. In "Branwen, daughter of Llyr" the prize is no longer a cauldron, but the maiden herself. During a battle between the Irish and the Welsh, Bran is wounded by a poisoned spear, and he commands his followers to cut off his head.

"Take my head, and carry it to the White Hill in London, and bury it there with the face towards France. You will be long on the road, and spend seven years feasting at Harddlech, with the Birds of Rhiannon singing to you, and the head will be as good a companion as it ever was." The magical head converses with and entertains its followers, until one of them contravenes the prohibitions that go with it, and they are obliged to leave their feasting, and bury it as ordered. "While the head was concealed, no plague came from across the sea to this island". (Trans. Jeffrey Gantz). The head was facing Europe, as a national guardian, the relic of a powerful king and Otherworld hero. The purpose of the Bath head was surely similar, a carving that showed the ancestral and sacred head cult in Celtic worship, but developed as a solar deity. It represented a civilised and evolved phase of the old worship, in which the barbarous elements of the nomadic head hunters had long since been turned into a religion connected with the flow of the seasons, and the head become identified with the Sun god.

The 'Gorgon's Head' should be seen as a god or hero, similar to Bran, a representative of the saving power of the Sun. The stylised hair and beard as flames, the wings and prominent staring eyes, the large ears, all show him to be a Sun God....fiery, flying through the air, seeing and hearing all that passes below his exaltation. The serpents around his neck are similar to those seen on various representations of native gods, and which were connected with fertility, and occasionally with water. The serpent, of course, is the animal of the Otherworld, as it hides in clefts in the rock close to the secrets of the Goddess.

One of the many additional pieces of evidence that can be offered from the interchange between the Celtic head cult and classical influence, is from Brittany, from the design of a coin minted during the 2nd century A.D. Referring to such coins in her lecture "Colonization of Brittany from Celtic Britain", Nora K Chadwick says: "Almost all show on the obverse a head which in far away Macedonia was the head of Appollo, crowned with a laurel wreath. But the Armorican coins have modified their models with the striking originality and beauty characteristic of Celtic art everywhere. The laurel wreath has become a coiffure of barbaric splendour, and the face has sacrificed Greek realism for design. There are some startling innovations. Of these the most interesting and distinctive are the tiny decapitated human heads attached to pearled cords issuing from the mouth and surrounding the head of this strange but still beautiful Appollo. Inevitably one calls to mind Posidonius's description of the Gaulish custom of cutting off and preserving the heads of their enemies, and again the famous passage of Lucan describing the picture of Ogmios, the Gaulish god of eloquence, drawing after him an eager group of men whose ears were attached to his tongue by fine gold chains." (Rhys Memorial Lecture, British Academy, 1965).

The Flaming Head

The Pattern of the Pediment

The remaining details of the Pediment give confirmation of the solar nature of the central head. The carvings of the pagan world are often thought of as 'idols', empty images to which foolish savages bowed and scraped and sacrificed their children. This is very far from the truth, as the carvings and statues served several different and meaningful functions, over and above that of being focal points for the power of the gods. The detailed beliefs of the people were shown in the old images, and they were intended to be "read", as each one portrayed a character or a myth from which a wealth of revealing magical, historical and religious information could be drawn. The images can still be read today, providing we have the initial insight into the Otherworld concepts from which they developed.

The head is mounted on a disc or shield, surrounded by a wreath of oak leaves. This not only shows him as a victor, but as a sun god. The oak was a magical tree to both the Romans and the Celts, and was closely identified with the principle of kingship. Such an identification is thought to have originated from the time when the oak was a food source, and important to survival. Druids worshipped in tree groves, and had especial reverence for the oak.

The fertility of the land itself was thought to be linked to the potency of the king, whose symbol was the oak tree. The pagan Irish actually killed and replaced their king if the land was not fertile; human sacrifices were intended to make contact with the Otherworld, and bring about an energy exchange for the benefit of all concerned. The oak was further identified with lightening, seen as the sky fire darting down to fertilise the earth, and so the classical thunderers Zeus and Jupiter were associated with the tree. The wreath of oak leaves is a statement of the identity of the hairy watcher....he is a victorious sun hero or sacred king, and is therefore a sun god.

The oak is also linked with a Celtic god Bel or Belenos, a solar being whose name means 'Brightly shining'. In folklore he was associated with the fertility of cattle, and his name is repeated in the Celtic feast of Beltaine, a fire festival that marked the coming of summer. This important day of life-awakening is still marked by the May Day celebrations in Britain and Europe, which occur on approximately the same date as the old feast. The traditional celebrations involve dancing, singing, drinking and licentious behaviour; the Padstow Hobby Horse being a good example of such a ritual still in operation. Little wonder that the Christians set the more controlled Archangel Michael to watch over the day, and the sacred hilltops where the solar worshipping fires were lit. The memory of this solar god Bel was so strong, that when St. George replaced St. Michael, after the English broke with the Roman Church during the reign of Henry 8th, George eventually began to appear in mummers plays and folk rituals, and occurs in the death and resurrection section of the Padstow ceremony. (For a more detailed discussion of this, see "Where is St. George ?" by Bob Stewart, Moonraker Press 1977).

Belenos was the Celtic Appollo, connected with the sun and with horses, and was a young and triumphant solar power of light. The carved head is more likely to be a head of Bel than of the monstrous Otherworld destroyer whom he and his divine brothers were supposed to control.

The supporting symbols of the Pediment present a coherent picture. It commences above the Head, with an eight pointed star. The disc or shield is held by two winged classical Victories. Below these are two sea beings, or Tritons, although very little of them remains. Immediately at the foot of these figures are one or two helmets, one of which bears an owl. The Victories stand upon spheres or balls, often interpreted as representing the world.

The entire sequence, as seen in the remaining stones, and as restored by comparison to similar carving and classical rules of proportion, is an indication of the order of the universe, as understood by the pagans.

Above is a star, the distant power of the heavenly bodies which were watched so closely by mankind. The main feature is the Sun, flying through the air on his round of the seasons. As he is supported by Victories who are associated with Minerva in classical symbolism, he is the Sun at midsummer, the glorious victor who has triumphed. Below him are the powers of the Sea, and below again are the powers of the Underworld, suggested by the Owl, bird of Hecate.

The pediment is a cosmology, a pattern that extends from the underworld or Otherworld to the stars. It can be further defined as a "Tree of Life", the general name for a group of pan-cultural symbols which all indicate an ascending or descending pattern of creation. The Roman/Greek pantheon is an obvious example of this pattern, and it occurs in Celtic, Norse, Mediterranean and Hebrew mythology. The forms are various, but the principle is the same. The key symbol ranges from a simple vegetative life and growth emblem or a phallic stone, right through the personalised orders of gods and goddesses from the underworld to the skies, to mathematical patterns. In this mathematical form we have the various types of knowledge attributed to Pythagoras and Plato, and the "Platonic Solids" which are the basis of the Qabalistic Tree of Life, used in magic from the medieval period the present day. Such efforts at integrated symbolism are the result of attempts to see the Universe as a harmonious or meaningful structure, an image which modern physics is still trying to prove in various ways. The urge to relate does not become lost, but merely changes its face according to the era.

A very useful comparison can be made between the Temple Pediment and the west front of the Abbey, only a few yards away. This shows us the same pattern, adapted to Christian symbolism, and with a strong emphasis on hierarchy and control through human agencies, which is quite unknown in the pagan carvings *(see photograph 6)*. At the top is God, and his power is seen descending through the mediation of his ministering angels, who clamber up and down ladders like medieval building workers. This power lights upon the King, who appoints the Bishops, who overlook the doorway through which the ordinary people enter.

A thousand years after the collapse of the Temple of Sulis Minerva, the ordinary

6. *The West Front of Bath Abbey. Here the "earth to heaven" concept first seen in the pagan Temple Pediment, is repeated, but with a Christian and authoritarian emphasis.*

folk were still illiterate, and still guided by visual carved symbols as definitions of the pattern that ruled their lives. The concept of "divine right of Kings" is clearly shown on the Abbey. This was inherited from the pagan times (although it traversed devious political and religious routes), when the King was literally the vessel of the Sun-god, responsible for the fertility of the land and the well-being of his people. This was echoed as late as the time of Charles the First of England, who lost his head, and hid in an oak tree. The country people identified his oak with various oak trees across England which were regarded with superstitious reverence.

The very stones of the Temple Pediment have brought us a lot closer to the identity of the "Gorgon's Head", but for the final evidence, we must turn to the eccentric chronicles of the Middle ages, and try to obtain some meaning from their jumble of folklore, myth, and history.

The Myth of King Bladud

Set into a niche, in the wall of the King's bath, is a small statue (*see photograph 9*). It is a seated man, with long hair, and a rather miserable face. He carries traces of blue paint. This figure was made in the 18th century, and is supposed to be the replacement for an earlier image which stood guard over the North gate of the city. The earlier figure, of wood, may have been a typical city totem or guardian, a common custom dating to a pagan origin. The famous Giants Gog and Magog were the traditional protectors of London, a city which abounds with totem figures. They were destroyed by fire, and their tradition was not kept up, like that of Bladud, although copies were taken to Australia in the last century.

Beneath the sad little figure, covered in pigeon droppings, forgotten and neglected, is his history; "Bladud, son of Lud Hudibras, 8th king of the Britons, first discoverer and founder of these Baths". The inscription was taken from a "History of the Kings of Britain", accepted for many centuries as fact, but which has little to offer in the way of acurate history. The 18th century figure of Bladud is the result of a popular movement of interest in ancient Britain, which had various effects upon the literature, architecture and scholarship of the country (and of Bath in particular), not all of which were beneficial. The core of the old tradition asserts that a British King, "Bladud", built the Baths and Temple, and that this action was not connected with the Romans. The tale has been ignored or dismissed in most works on Aquae Sulis, as the Romans very definitely *were* responsible, yet it can be shown that it fits very well indeed with the remains that we can see today. Bladud, (the father of the unfortunate King Lear made famous by Shakespeare, who drew several of his plots from native tradition), has a strong claim as the founder of the site, but not by any means as a true or historical person!

The statue that is said to have guarded the old city of Bath, and its copy now sitting glumbly over the site of the Roman enclosure of the sacred spring, are both descendants of the solar being who rose up over the Temple of Sulis Minerva....and they can all be said to be "King Bladud".

The myth of King Bladud was set out by Geoffrey of Monmouth, writing in the reign of Henry 2nd. Geoffrey aimed to arrange a coherent genealogy of the British Kings, and the earlier stages are obviously filled out with folklore, myth, and other curious and non-factual material, which may seem rather unsatisfactory to the prosaic historian. The author was attempting to prove a continuous line for Royalty up to the Saxon period. These proofs were often attempts to satisfy the vanity of the ruling family of the day; and were certainly an important part of the medieval passion for rewriting history as an honourable and linear progression, rather than as an uncoherent mess of tyranny and oppression.

There are some additional and more subtle reasons for this obsession with genealogy, which are direct descendants of pre-Christian belief. The pagan kings were supposed to be vessels of the god-power, a process which eventually became hereditary, to be passed down through recognised bloodlines, often established by matrilinear descent. To preserve knowledge of origins, all primitive people work out long memorised family lists which are learned for many generations. In time this function becomes the speciality of the priesthood, although we know that nobles were expected to recite their ancestors' names in the heroic structure of early Irish culture which had a well defined Druid caste. The same process is found in the Old Testament, and in the two proofs of the descent of Jesus Christ in the New Testament (one matrilinear, and one patrilinear).

The pseudo-historical genealogies, such as that compiled by Geoffrey, were the last remnants of this type of magical proof of descent, and were written at a time when factual history was still blurred into myth, and had only seen the merest beginnings of political "cooking" outside the religious sphere. A 12th century writer would have drawn on some factual material, a great deal of oral traditional lore, and the written chronicles and books, classical and native, which were in circulation at the time. From this hotchpotch of sources, he would have to compile something honourable, flattering, and religiously inoffensive. In Geoffrey's case this was supposed to prove that the Britons originated with Brutus, a descendant of the fleeing Aeneas of Troy, who founded the fire temple of Vesta in Rome. Within this would-be-classical proof, a lot of valuable ancient lore has been kept, and a surprising amount of pagan myth and magical symbolism may be found without effort.

Geoffrey is often quoted as the primary source of all the later printed Chronicles, which faithfully preserved this false history for several centuries. His material, however, was taken from two written sources, already in existence.

"Walter, Archdeacon of Oxford, a man of great eloquence and learning in foreign histories, offered me a very ancient book in the British tongue, which in a continued and regular Story and elegant Stile, related the actions of them all (The British Kings) from Brutus, the first King of the Britons, down to Cadwallader, the son of Cadwallo...." (The British History, translated into English from the Latin of Geoffrey of Monmouth, by Aaron Thompson, 1718). This book was found in Armorica (Brittanny), and Geoffrey translated it from the Old Welsh or a similar native tongue, into the formal Latin of his profession. Another source, obviously derived from the same tradition or oral history as Geoffrey, was the Welsh chronicle of Tysilio, to which he probably had access.

"Blaiddyd, the son of Rhun, came next to the throne, and reigned 20 years. He built Caervaddon (Bath) and formed there a warm unguent to be a perpetual remedy for the diseased. Moreover, by sacrificing to the enchantress Minerva, he kindled an inextinguishable fire there, which when it burned out, rekindled in balls of fire. This was done about the time, when in consequence of Elijahs prayer, there was no rain for three years and six months. Blaiddyd was also active in scientific pursuits, he was the first who introduced the magic art into Britain, nor did he cease in such studies until essaying to fly with a pair of wings, which he had invented, he fell down on the Temple of Appollo in London, and was dashed to pieces". (Tysilio's Chronicle, trans. Rev. Peter Roberts, 1811).

This version of the tale, incidentally, gives us another major reason for the

62

construction of the old chronicles, in its reference to the Old Testament prophets. The sequence of the known history of the World was deliberately made to fit the calculations devised by church authorities. All pre-Christian historical knowledge was compressed, or suppressed, to fit the assumed dates in the Old Testament. The Chronicle version of classical and native history mingled together, formed a strange bridge between the writings of the ancient world and the traditional lore of the common people, in a manner which was acceptable to the learned and pious reader....who would be familar with a little of each.

Geoffrey himself makes small differences within Bladud's story as set out by Tysilio, stating: "After Hurdibras came his son Baldudus, who reigned for twenty years, and built the city of Kaerbadus, now called Bath. In it he built warm baths for the curing of diseases. He made Minerva patron of the Baths, and in her Temple placed inexhaustible fires — these never burned down to ashes, but as soon as they began to fail, were turned into balls of stone. Baldudus was a man of great ingenuity, and taught necromancy throughout Britain, continually doing many wonderful deeds, and finally making himself wings to fly through the upper air. But he fell onto the Temple of Appollo in Ternova, his body being broken into many pieces". Geoffrey's translator has kept the original rendering of Ternova (Troya Nova) which was supposed to be London. London was connected with Brutus, the assumed founder of Britain, who was a descendant of the Trojan Aeneas, hence the name of Troya Nova. The myth is a typical 'after the cataclysm' theme, where legendary founders are fleeing from a disaster to commence a new culture. Celtic lore in particular abounds with this theme, so much so that many writers have suggested it has some ancient historical origin. The mighty Alexander the Great was told by a Celt that the Celtic people feared nothing, unless it be that the sea rise up to overwhelm them, or that the sky should fall on their heads. Oaths were sworn to this formula, and the "disaster" theme perpetuated by the myth of Brutus is merely an attempt to 'Latinise' a type of story common in the oral tradition of the time.

A rather odd aspect of the "New Troy" tradition is that the old prehistoric mazes, supposed to be of ritual origin, were called "Troytowns" by the English country people. Is this the result of Geoffrey's chronicle passing into general education? The sites referred to were locations for folk ceremonies of dancing and pattern walking, of a type which is done in parts of Brittany even today. These ritual patterns must have been handed down from an uncertain pagan source, in much the same way as the story of Bladud survived, but only *he* got into print, to be preserved. His story has all the hallmarks of a myth, such as that of Icarus who flew too close to the Sun through pride and had his cunningly made wings melted.

Geoffrey was also drawing upon the earlier account of Solinus, who wrote in the 3rd century, describing the hot springs and saying that they were presided over by Minerva, with her fire. The entire story retained its content in print as late as the 16th century, when Holinshed's Chronicle of 1577 tells us: "Baldud, son of Lud Hudibras, began to rule over the Britons in the year of the World 3085 (referring to the Christian calculations). This man was well learned in the science of astronomy and of necromancy, by which as common report sayeth, he made the hot baths in

63

7. *A restoration of the Temple Pediment, built in Sydney Gardens, Bath. The design is hopelessly out of keeping with the classical principles made clear in the reconstruction given by Cunliffe and Richmond and Toynbee, and has distinctly been influenced by the "Gorgon" theory, to such an extent that the head carved here is full of writhing snakes, which are not present upon the original.*

the city of Caervian, which is now called Bath. But William of Malmesbury is of the contrary opinion, affirming that Julius Ceasar made these baths, or rather repaired them when he was here in England, which is not like to be true, for Julius Ceasar, as by good conjecture we have to think, never came so far within the land that way forth...."

This shows an interesting development of the theme, support for a Roman origin of the site as opposed to a British one, at a time when there was no archaeological evidence available (nor was there any archaeology!). This situation is rather similar to the popular knowledge of Bath today, when very few people realise the Celtic or native affinities of the site which greatly add to its singificance. Yet both sides of the picture are quite valid, despite William of Malmesbury's vindictive alteration of history. The 'Ceasar' version gives us the Roman element, while the 'Baldud' one gives us the Celtic element. Of course each story is absurd as history, but each is correct in essence. Holinshed refers to "common report", which is the oral tradition, thus affirming the validity of his additions in the usual manner by saying that he did not make them up, but took them from an existing source known to the people.

The reader will have seen already that there is a similarity between King Bladud's flight and his link with the Temple of Appollo, and the basic pattern of the Temple pediment discovered in 1790.

The dedication to Minerva and the practice of magic are clear references to the pagan origins of the site, even though the remains were buried at the time that Geoffrey and his subsequent fellow-chroniclers were writing.

Appollo, with whom Bladud is linked, has an interesting history, and modern scholars state that he is not a native Greek god at all, but of northern origin. He is certainly the Bel or Belenos of the Celts, who were renowned throughout the classical world as the main worshippers of Appollo. Linguistically, Appollo, Belenos and Baal are related 'god-words'. There is a famous classical quotation from Hecateus' lost book "a Circuit of the Earth" (approximately 500 B.C.), given by Diodorus. He says that the Greeks link Appollo with the Hyperborean lands (Lands at the back of the North Winds), as his mother Leto was born there. He goes on to describe a country that may be Britain, as it is small, and situated opposite the mainland of Gaul (ie opposite France and Belgium). In this Hyperborean land was a circular Temple of stone, dedicated to Appollo himself, to which he returned in person every nineteen years. This sounds very much like Stonehenge, built upon calculations of the passage of the Sun and planets and stars.

This intriguing passage presents several interesting elements. The term of nineteen years is actually the figure well known as the period required for the moon to return to synchronicity within the solar year. It is also close to the period of time that passes between solar eclipses. Hecateus also mentions that the Hyperboreans welcome the god with music and dancing, playing upon the harp. It should be remembered, however, that Britain abounds with stone circles, other than Stonehenge. The solar and lunar alignments of Stonehenge are well known, although fine details are still the subject of discussion (see 'The Stone Circles of the British Isles' Aubrey Burl, Yale University, for a detailed examination of the subject).

It is not surprising to find symbols and dedications of Diana/Artemis and Appollo connected in various ways with Bath, as he links healing, fertility, life and death, and the brightly shining Sun.

The tradition has preserved, in its dreamlike manner, the same story that the patient work of the modern archaeologists has revealed to us. A sun-king or god, working magic, flying through the air on wings, linked to both classical and native roots.

Bale's Chronicle of 1548 expands the story further, with siginificant comments: "While still a youth, Bladud the Great, 10th King of Britain, spent much time in Athens in Greece, in order to make a careful study of philosophy. On the death of his father Ruthhudibras, he returned home after several years of study, bringing with him teachers of the four principle sciences that for the future his kingdom might enjoy the advantage of their instructions. According to Merlin, he founded a school of literature for these men at Stamford, that they might there teach the liberal arts, and to it they drew a considerable audience. Bladud himself was skilled in the profane learning of the Gentiles, being an especially diligent student of the stars. Writers say that he founded the city of Bath, and with remarkable skill built in it hot baths, which are still in existence. That the springs might never fail, he made Minerva the patron goddess of the place, and built a temple in her honour; he also spread necromancy throughout almost the whole country. This story, however, I judge to be wholly false, for just as some baths are made hot by art, so others are so naturally, for the water, as Basilius and Bede tell us, makes its way through channels in the earth, and then spouting out from mine-workings, boils.

King Bladud is said to have written several books about mathematical magic and to have left other proofs of the keenness of his intellect. According to Virunnius, he used, like a second Proteus, to assume various shapes and to disturb the elements with strange quakings from the earth. Last of all, having by magic spell obtained wings, he essayed to fly into the air in sight of the people and fell headlong on the Temple of Appollo. This happened in the 21st years of his reign. He was so grievously injured by the fall that he died, and was buried at Trenovantum...."

The prosaic explanation of the source of the hot waters is very close to the latest modern theory, that the waters are heated by movement through the surrounding strata, over an immense period of time. With expansions credited to Merlin and Virunnius, both notorious source of old magical lore, Bales' version of the story adds a little more to our evidence.

The Chronicle descriptions of Bladud state that he practised and taught the following arts or sciences:

1. Astronomy/Astrology.
2. Necromancy.
3. Fire Magic.
4. Shape Changing.
5. Therapy.
6. Flying through the air by magical means.

8. *Ritual mask, from the Temple area. This mask bears a close resemblance to similar items found in Europe, and is very near in style to the traditional ritual mask used in the Padstow May ceremony. The Padstow ceremony, a folk custom of undoubted pagan origin, includes a death-and resurrection sequence, the character St. George (who is a rationalisation of a sun-god), and until only a few years ago, involved reverence of a spring and water source. Such traditional ceremonies often provide an insight into early religious practices, particularly when they are compared to classical references.*

These are all typical of the practices of the pagan priesthoods and mythical heroes. Bladud's magic is exactly that of the Druids, as shown in the Irish and Welsh sources and classical descriptions. He is a priest king in a typically Celtic or British manner. This is what we would expect when we remember that his story originally comes from Welsh and Breton sources, as these countries shared a common racial heritage.

The Chronicle of John Hardygne, 1543, gives yet another slight difference to the tale.

"Bladud king of Britain had Logres and Albany (ie Brittany and England). He made a university and a study at Stamford, and a flame and his Temple at Bath his city, which university dured to the coming of Saint Augustine, and the Bishop of Rome interdited it for heresies that fell among the Saxons and Britons together mixed....

.... In Caer Bladim he made a temple right
And set a flamyne theirein to gouerne
And afterwards a Fetherham he dight
And sett To fly with wings, as he could best discerene,
Aboue the ayre nothying hym to werne
He flyed on high to the temple Apolyne
And there brake his neck, for al his great doctrine."

In other words the pagan tradition, exemplified by the teachings of Bladud, survived until the arrival of Augustine the reformed rake and libertine, in 597 A.D. This is not a literal reference to history, but comes pretty close to it, as Augustine's main concern was not the saving of pagan souls, but the destruction of rival and older branches of the Christian cult which were mingled with native traditions. The great controversy of the "Pelagian heresy" was started by one Pelagius, a Celt. He claimed that mankind could save their own souls by effort, but the Latin Church decreed original sin. Pelagius' doctrine is exactly that of the heroic Otherworld raid, in which the benefits of the divine realms were accessible through effort and courage, and not merely doled out for obedience.

"Bladud" is the epitome of a religious and cultural hero and educator, and symbolically his effect was felt into Christian times, for as long as the older Celtic heritage resisted. He represents the pagan lore and worship, cropping up again and again in curious and unexpected places, gathering to himself all sorts of attributes and subtle twists, none of them truly historical, but all valuable as cultural and mythical material.

Bladud bears a close resemblance to the Biblical character Simon Magus, mentioned in the Acts of the Apostles. Simon was a native of Samaria, and claimed to be an *aeon*, a highly powerful spirit, part of the hierarchy of the Gnostics, a mysterious sect who merged various aspects of Christianity with pagan and eastern cult practices and ritual magic. He is famous for offering money to the Apostles, but was duly refused a deal on their magical powers by the indignant Peter. He gathered a following for himself, in competition, and kept a beautiful woman who he suggested was a reincarnation of Helen of Troy, Minerva, or the mother goddess of Wisdom, Sophia. He then built a device to fly in the air, but crash landed at Rome, much like Bladud or Icarus before him.

Simon's character and story seem to have been heavily edited, but his place in the Gospel is probably that of the magical pagan competitor, possibly an actual historical leader of a rival cult that could have eclipsed early Christianity.

In Irish legend, we have the Druid Mac Ruith (Son of the Wheel). He used his powers to make a flying machine, which soared through the heavens and was dashed to pieces. The wheel was called the "Ruith Fail" or Wheel of light.

So Bladud has the solar imagery of the sun flying through the air, and crashes at Winter. Simon Magus and Mac Ruith are obviously the same sort of character, altered for different audiences. Who is the king who makes a perpetual fire, and rises into the sky, only to land on the Temple of Appollo? Surely he is "Appollo" himself.

If we look at the elements of the King's name, we find that it is made of Bal or Bel, and then Dud or Dydd. He is therefore a priest of Bel, for the name is derived from Bel and Derwdd (the sun god and the druid). Baldud or Bladud or Blaidydd is the burning sun-face of the Temple pediment, and although he has been dashed to pieces (like the Egyptian sun god Osiris who was cut up into little bits) we can begin to put him back into his rightful place.

The popularity of Bladud is shown in yet another tale, from a traditional source, which was first published in Dr. Pierces "Memoirs" of 1697. He was a physician in Bath, and encountered this local tradition at first hand.

The basic story was that Bladud contracted leprosy while abroad, and on his return, took a job as a swineherd to save himself from being confined by his father. He noticed that the pigs bathed their scabby skins in a nearby steamy swamp, and so decided to try it himself. The cure was effective, and he returned to his fathers' court. In time he became king, and dedicated the baths and temple in memory of his miraculous cure.

The story is a typical myth. Bladud is a diseased prince, who is risking imprisonment by his father. He cannot rule, because he is imperfect. He is the same as the maimed Fisher King in the Holy Grail stories, and as Bran of the Pierced Thighs, mentioned earlier in the context of the severed head. They are rulers who cannot rule because of disease or lack of virility, and their only cure is from the Otherworld. The theme is that of the renewal of the Sun in Winter, the magic of death and renewed life, and a symbol of the negative aspects of the human psyche. The Sun was renewed in the magical cauldron of the Otherworld, and Bladud was cured in the swamp where the hot springs arise.

It is very significant that he is led to the water by pigs, for the pig was the totem animal of the Otherworld to the Celts. The Welsh goddess Keridwen, similar to the fierce primitive Mother Goddesses generally known, had the sow or pig as her special beast. It was very fertile, it ate its young, and was the ideal prolific food animal. There are many similar stories of sacred sites being founded by the acts of totem birds and animals. Rome itself had such a tale, and the animals reveal the nature of the god or goddess connected with the site, often in the most primitve aspect.

In 'Pagan Celtic Britain', Dr. Ross states...."The boar is, without doubt, the cult animal par excellence of the Celts....

"In the literatures of the Celtic world, the boar is represented in a variety of ways. The role of the beast as an important culinary element in the sacred ritual of the Otherworld feast, as well as in more mundane festivals, as suggested by the evidence from graves, where the placing of joints of pork beside the elaborately equipped chieftains indicates that this was intended to be food for the feast beyond the grave, is borne out to a striking degree in the Irish tales. Here pork is the proper food to be served at the feast and in the ritual of hospitality in the court of kings, and in the dwellings of the gods. It also figures in Irish mythology as a prognostic animal, while the insular literatures are full of references to beings metamorphosed in pig form, and to great supernatural Otherworld pigs which bring a trail of death and disaster behind them....Perhaps the role of divine swineherd stemmed from the concept of an original swine-god, protector of the animals, and capable of taking on their form"

The complete story of the pigs that lead Bladud: from Robert Pierce M.D., in 1713, as follows:

"Bladud, eldest son of *Lud-Hudibras*, (then King of *Britain* and eighth from *Brute*) having spent eleven years at *Athens* in the Study of the Liberal Arts and Sciences (that City being in those Days the chief Academy, not only of *Greece*, but of this part of the World also) came home a *Leper*, whither from that hotter Climate he had conversed in, or from ill Diet, or Infection, it doth not appear, those unlettter'd times giving down little or no Account of things (though of greater moment) then transacted; but a *Leper* he was, and for that reason shut up, that he might not infect others. He, impatient of this Confinement, chose rather a mean Liberty than a Royal Restraint, and contrived his Escape in Disguise, and went very remote from his Father's Court, and into an untravell'd part of the Country, and offers his Service in any common Imployment; thinking it (probably) likelier to be undiscover'd under such mean Circumstances than greater. He was entertain'd in Service at Swainswicke (a small Village, two Miles from this City) his Business (amongst other things) was to take Care of the Pigs, which he was to drive from place to place, for their Advantage in Feeding upon Beachmasts, Acorns, and Haws &c. the Hills hereabouts then abounding with such Trees, tho' now few, of the two first, remain. Yet there is a Hill, close upon the *South* Part of this City, that still retains the name of *Beachen Cliff*, tho' there is scarcely a Beach-Tree left upon it.

He thus driving his Swine from place to place, observ'd some of the Herd, in very cold Weather, to go down from the Side of the Hill into an *Alder-moore*, and thence return, cover'd with black Mud. Being a Thinking Person, he was very solicitous to find out the reason why the Pigs that wallow in the Mire in the Summer, to cool

71

themselves, should do the same in Winter; he observ'd them farther, and following them down, he at length perceiv'd a Steam and Smoak to arise from the place where the Swine wallow'd. He makes a way to it, and found it to be warm; and this satisfied him that for the Benefit of this Heat the Pigs resorted thither.

He being a *Virtuoso*, made farther Observation; that whereas those filthy Creatures, by their foul Feeding, and nasty Lying, are subject to Scabs, and foul Scurfs, and Eruptions on their Skin, some of his Herd that were so, after a while, became whole and smooth, by their often wallowing in this Mud.

Upon this he considers with himself, why he should not receive the same Benefit by the same Means; he trys it, and succeeded in it; and when he found himself cured of his *Leprosie*, declares who he was; his Master was not apt to believe him, at first, but at length did, and went with him to Court, where he (after a while) was owned to be the King's Son, and after his Father's Death succeeded him in the Government, and built this City, and made these *Baths*."

The Ancient Book

The origin of Geoffrey's 'ancient book' is still the subject of argument, as the book itself has never been found. Some scholars maintain that his entire reference to the book is a fiction, or a literary concept typical of the old chronicles, asserting an ancient origin as proof of truthfulness.

As far as the present discussion of King Bladud is concerned, the truthfulness of the source is almost irrelevant, because it is the mythical content of the story, set out in the first half of the 12th century that is important. We can judge Bladud by his *actions* in the History, then compare him to others who acted in the same way and performed the same type of magic. Even if Geoffrey fabricated the 'ancient book', his History of the British Kings abounds with mythical material that was common to the Celts in Brittany and Wales and the West of England, from whence the Bretons had partially derived, by emigration and cultural exchange over a long period of time.

Geoffrey is also, of course, the major source for the material on King Arthur, and has had an immense influence through this and his other characters on the development of English literature. It hardly needs to be said nowadays that Arthur, too, is far more than a distortion of a British king who may or may not have existed!

The Chronicle of Tysilio is mentioned in connection with Geoffrey's sources (*Levis, the British King who tried to fly, page 12*).

"One of the most interesting modern contributions to this fascinating and elusive subject is a paper read before the British Academy, 7 November 1917, by W.M. Flinders Petrie, F.R.S., entitled 'Neglected British History', in which he calls specific attention to Tysilio's Chronicle...."

The gist of this paper was that Tysilio pre-dated Geoffrey, but is hardly ever mentioned as one of his possible sources. Once again, the dating of the tales is not important to this discussion, though it is extremely important in the broader

9. *The statue of King Bladud over the "Kings Bath", above the source of the main hot Spring. This statue was said to have replaced an older city effigy, a custom common to many cities, which dates back to pagan belief in the power of guardian images connected with distinct localities.*

73

history of literature; what really counts is that such stories were (fortunately) set down in writing, and so preserved recognisable native traditions which have clear pagan affinities.

Although scholars can argue for ever about the *exact* sources of Geoffrey's material, hardly anyone would suggest that he merely fantasised all of it, there are too many older native traditions that are obviously one and the same as those mentioned in his "History" or his 'Prophecies of Merlin' or 'Life of Merlin'.

As far as his reference to Bath is concerned, we have the support of earlier writers, such as Solinus, and the Irish version of Bladud in the tale of the Druid Mac Roth. Geoffrey's contribution is likely to be the latter part of a coherent myth which has various solar associations. The folk tale of the pigs, is likely to be an earlier part of the same story, as is suggested in the section on the reconstruction of the myth — "King Bladud Restored" (*page 59*).

The special value of Geoffrey's version of the 'Bath myth' is that he cites the name of Bladud, as does Tysilio, giving the magical attributes of this character over and above the dedication of the Temple to Minerva which had already been written about by Solinus, who was possibly writing during the period of Temple use. Additionally, as the derivation of the name suggests, Geoffrey used his 'ancient book' and his knowledge of the native tongue to cunningly poke fun at other scholars. At the conclusion of his History, he writes that he will leave the history of the Kings of the Saxons to William of Malmesbury, or to Henry Huntingdon: "But I advise them to be silent concerning the kings of the Britons, since they have not that book in the British tongue, which Walter Archdeacon of Oxford brought out of Brittany". This statement is not only a proof of his superior sources (something beloved of scholars through the ages) but is very reminiscent of the Celtic scorn for the non-Celtic speaking people. This superior attitude, no doubt stemming from long centuries of intense persecution, is still manifest in parts of Wales and Ireland today, where people will revert to the native tongue in the presence of strangers.

Geoffrey's History appeared some time after 1130, being the first book that set out the material of British myth in Latin (disregarding the book in Breton that Geoffrey says was his source). Prior to his work, no material of this sort existed in written form, but by 1155 the History was translated into French by the Jersey poet Wace, a Norman, as the 'Roman de Brut' (the Romance of Brutus, Geoffrey's legendary founder of Britain). By 1190 a large amount of related material had appeared; the romances of Chrétien de Troyes, the Tristan romances, and the lays of Marie de France. Further material was to follow in the forms of 'Lancelot', 'The Quest of the Holy Grail', and 'The Death of King Arthur', all from unknown authors. Geoffrey's 'History of the Kings of Britain', and his later books, seem to have marked a turning point in the appearance and acceptability of native myth and lore among the educated classes. Furthermore, from Geoffrey's reworking of old material, a new order of spiritual literature was born, for the tales of King Arthur and the Holy Grail combined ancient roots and primitive symbols of Celtic origin with the highest aspirations of the age, represented by the Grail itself.

For a further insight into Geoffrey's sense of humour, we should consider the actual origins, or possible derivations, of the name 'baldud' or 'bladud' in detail.

The linguistic argument

The two sections on the possible derivation of the words 'Sulis' and 'Bladud', look into the linguistic possibilities of their origins, with a particular emphasis on the Celtic languages. In each case, this emphasis is justified by the structure of the words themselves, and by their use in connection with Aquae Sulis. The classical and strictly Latin possibilities have not been passed over, however, and Latin origins and relationships have been considered, both in the special sections on the 'god-names' and through the whole argument of the rest of the book.

The method of deriving information from a broad translation and interpretation of ancient names, connected with particular places or practices, is very well established within the fields of folklore, mythological studies, and archaeology, although interpretations range from being extremely cautious to wildly imaginative. The argument given here travels a middle road between those two extremes, tending towards the cautious! Most of the linguistic material suggested is very well known and accepted nowadays, and can be confirmed from any number of research works on the Celtic and Latin languages, as well as by the archaeological reference sources and specific Celtic studies which are readily available for anyone wishing to take the matter further. Indeed, the whole linguistic argument demands research, and could be given a more detailed analysis in its own right....the reader will see that there are some curious parallels between Latin and Celtic languages *and* symbolism at Aquae Sulis which are not likely to be mere coincidences. Although they are all dealt with through our text in various places, a summary of their relationship would be as follows:

*Bla*dud or *Bel*dud built a Temple to Minerva, also called *Bel*isima; Minerva was closely related to a Celtic goddess, *Brig*idda, and all of these terms come down to the meaning 'bright' 'light' or 'shining'. *Bla*dud crashed on the Temple of *Appollo* the god of the *sun*, and there has been some confusion between *Sulis* and *Sol* or *Solis* the Latin word for the *Sun*. Contemporary evidence (such as the Antonine Itinerary and actual inscriptions on the site) show that the springs were presided over by the Goddess *Sulis*, who was equated with *Minerva* (no god Sul is ever mentioned, except in modern writings, incidentally). *Sulis* is probably a native word, meaning hole or gap (from which the waters come), but a Latin word *Suillis* means 'pertaining to pigs'. King *Bladud* is led to the hot springs by *Pigs*, which were the magical animal of the Otherworld, and the totem beast of a Celtic goddess. So magical to the Celts were pigs, that they were explained as coming from the Otherworld or Underworld, i.e. *from beneath the ground.*

The usual way of accounting for these mergings between the god-names is to find a common linguistic origin, and the basic argument that was put forward by many writers, which is generally accepted, is that the Celts and the Romans ultimately derive from the same 'Indo European' roots. But the connection is not nearly as simple as a mere verbal link, for it is *conceptual*, and is closely interwoven with the myth of 'The Hero who slays a Monster', and his protection by a Goddess. At this level of awareness, we are approaching the primitive roots of all language,

76

which are essentially magical, in which the *name* of any particular thing *is the thing itself*. At this 'unconscious' state of magical naming, the dreamlike merging of the Celtic and Latin terms, and their symbolism, begins to make sense. It is very likely that this magical sense was natural to the mixture of peoples who came to Aquae Sulis, as it was inherent in the worship and everyday life of their cultures. It only seems 'coincidental' in modern retrospect, and the linguistic similarities would have been evidence of the universality of the gods, as far as the pagans were concerned.

There is absolutely no suggestion, by the way, of any planned or conscious integration or overall system of worship that spread across Europe, nor any hint of an 'underground' or 'occult' link between the different cults. The relationship was *organic*, a natural growth of thousands of years of nature worship by people with common origins. Bearing this in mind, the derivation of the words is certainly valuable, but is not the centre of the argument!

Even if we had no name from inscription for 'Sulis', and no name for Geoffrey's founder of Bath, the basic interpretation of the site would remain viable through the *attributes* and the archaeological finds related to the cultural background of the Celts and Romans. The meaning of the names themselves is supportive evidence, not conclusive proof. The only real proof is the site itself, and the carvings that are visible, and these in themselves show the essential elements of Springs, and primary Male and Female powers (the 'Gorgon's Head' and the 'Luna Pediment') with various other divine and heroic connections on altars and other carvings. We are fortunate indeed to have Geoffrey's History and Pierce's Memoirs to give us additional literary support to the theory of the myth....but its units are already visible on the site.

Derivation of the word "Bladud"

Both 'Bladud' and 'Sulis' belong to the curious group of 'god-names' which occur in early inscription and literature. As such, they have linguistic roots which may be traced, and the names themselves generally refer back to the nature or function of the deity.

Unlike the word 'Sulis' which we have in a constant form from inscription, 'Bladud' exists in several variants, due to a long history of copying, both in manuscript and in print. The variants are due to the general freedom of spelling that was common in chronicles, especially when words or names were being transposed (rather than translated) from one language to another. Changes also occured because of different copying, and later due to a simple shortage of print, when repetitions were made on the same page, but using whatever approximate means of spelling came to hand.

The variants of Bladud are: BLAIDYDD, BLADUD, BLADUTH, BALDUD, BELDUD, BLADUS, BLEDUD. Geoffrey uses the name more than once, calling other supposed kings by it, or by close variants, such as Belduno or Blegabred. "This last prince for songs and skill in all musical instruments excelled all the musicians that had been before him, so he seemed worthy of the title of *The God of Jesters"* *(Geoffrey, History, iii, 19)*.

The differences of spelling do not affect the root of the word, 'Bla, Bal, or Bel', which is a word constantly associated with 'Brightness' and 'Fire'. "BEL" was an ancient word for the god of light or fire, known in various forms throughout the Celtic and the classical realms, and is related to the "Baal" mentioned in the Bible, to Bel, and to other near-eastern deities. (Even the name of the sun god adopted by the Greeks, "Appollo", was originally "Appello", and it has been suggested by various writers as having the 'bel' root within it, which would not be too surprising when we consider his attributes).

The Celtic feast of Beltinne or Beltaine has already been mentioned, which involved fire rituals, purification, and the ritual rebirth of the Sun. In old Scots 'Bele' meant 'fire', and the word still has meaning today in various derivations and languages as 'beautiful'.

Other associated words that are worth considering are:
BALDORDDUS: Welsh — 'Babbling'
BLADHM: Irish — 'Flame'. (In John Hardynge's Chronicle, Bath is referred to as 'Caer Bladim', and Geoffrey's 'Blegabred' is changed to 'Bladud Gabred', which suggests that Hardynge had some knowledge of the language, such as Welsh).

It is likely that Geoffrey of Monmouth is making one of his many learned jokes, when he refers to "Bladud" and "Blegabred" in connection with fire, music, jesting, therapy and the other magical attributes, for there is considerable linguistic interplay that refers us back again and again to the mythological origins. The words 'Blad' and 'Blag' also mean 'an enormous mouth' or 'a babbler', and to an educated author who had Welsh as a native language, the interplay would not have been lost, but quite obvious. Whether or not he was aware of the pagan origin of this 'folk' material is of course another matter altogether, but he has taken an old traditional source, amplified it into a joke, and still left the meaning intact. It is tempting to think of Geoffrey's 'History' and other works, as a 'ludibrium', or silly story which embodies mythical or mystical truths; certainly his adaptation of Arthur developed into such.

The second part of the word Bladud, has the following possible Celtic derivations:
DYDD: Welsh — 'Day'
DUD: Gaelic — 'A word or sound/gloomy and black' (Irish: DUBH)
DIA: Irish and Gaelic — 'A god'

From the Welsh 'Dydd' derive:
DYDDIO: 'To judge or reconcile'
DYDDIWR: 'Mediator or arbitrator'

Another possible area of derivation may be:
DRUIDA: Gaulish
DRYW: Welsh
DRUWID or DERWYDD: It hardly needs to be said that a root word of this sort is the

78

origin of our modern term 'Druid' derived from classical sources, and 'dryw' still means 'seer' in Welsh today.

Either of these areas of derivation would suggest that the second part of the name either means 'a god' or alternatively 'a druid'. As Bladud behaves exactly like both a god *and* a Druid (or mediator of Otherworld powers) we can take our pick....and still appreciate Geoffrey's subtle pun. Finally, there is one other possible connection with the word 'dud', which may be of value or significance. In Scots Gaelic, the word 'dud' means 'gloomy or black', with particular reference to Winter.

"In Wales, January was called 'the black month'. November, the first month of winter, was known as the dark or black month in Scotland, Cornwall and Brittany, and the Scots referred to the depths of winter as '*an Dudlachd*', 'gloom'. It was the season of the '*death* revels' presided over by a 'king' with a blackened face, whose emblem of office was a sword, scythe or sickle" (*A & B Rees, Celtic Heritage, page 84*). If the 'dud' part of the name refers to Winter, it could relate to the above type of belief. To refer to a hero-king or solar deity as 'bright-dark' would be a typical example of Celtic duality in concept, and would again fit Bladud's career of glory and then ignominy.

The interesting point about the derivations of god-names in general, and of the words 'Sulis' and 'Bladud' in particular, is that they could have been nonsense through linguistic derivation....but they were not! It is so common for god names to make sense, that their sensible derivations and appropriate meanings are hardly ever commented upon. The chances of a god-name deriving from a meaningless or inappropriate term are very small indeed, so it would actually be *more* surprising for Bladud to mean, 'cake crust' or 'boot mud' than for it to mean 'bright god' 'bright priest' or 'bright-dark'. The *coincidences* involved are not coincidental at all, they are re-enforcements of the natural qualities of the deities, expressed as proper names.

The name "Vlatos" appears on Belgic coins, struck not long after Julius Caesar's conquest of Gaul. These coins curiously feature a male head, with wings and a torque, the Celtic symbol of royalty. As our name 'Bladud' would have been pronounced Vla-thuth, the coin may be a further indication that this word was a term or *title* used not only as a god name, but as a king-name. The Celtic kings were considered to be the manifestations of the god-power, as we know from Irish lore. Whoever struck the coins marked 'Vlatos Atevla' was probably a leader of mercenary troops, as the coins are Roman-style copies, with Celtic imagery. It may be that the term Vlathuth or Bladud was a widespread god-king title; certainly we find it associated with a leader in Gaul who struck coins, shown as a torque bearer with wings, and it is possibly related to the winged and torque bearing head carved at Aquae Sulis, if we accept the evidence that this is indeed one and the same being as Geoffrey's 'King Bladud'. (See also Bob Stewart, "The Myth of King Bladud" Bath 1980).

The Derivation of the word "Sulis"

The word "Sulis" has been suggested as a Celtic derivation, a proper name which originates as the description of the source of the Hot Springs. Given time, names of this sort become inseparable from the attributes and personality of the presiding deity of any site, and the dedications to "the Goddess Sulis" from the Roman period show a clear identification, always feminine.

In Irish: SUIL — (f) 'An eye'. Also used as meaning eye or hole (of a strap).
In Gaelic: SUIL — 'An eye'. The centre of a whirlpool. An opening or orifice.
SUILEATH: 'Sharp sighted and knowing'
In Manx: SHILLEY or SOOIL: 'An eye'

In modern Welsh the term is missing, but in Old Welsh, it corresponded to the terms given.

The English verb "to swallow" is derived from the same source, and is related to an Icelandic word meaning "whirlpool". (*Note the term 'swallow' for drain, and 'Swallow holes' in caving terminology*).

In modern Welsh the term "Dydd Sul" is used for Sunday, but this is not of Celtic origin, but taken from an adaptation of the Latin "Deis Solis". The root Sul is not necessarily cognate with Sol, from the Latin, although the similarity of the two has caused some confusion in writers who have described "the god SUL". Presumably they have confused the solar identity of the 'Gorgon's Head', forgetting that the inscriptions are always to the *goddess* SULIS.

A word SUILLUS exists in Latin, which means 'of or belonging to Swine'. While it is tempting to think that this may mean that the goddess' name refers to the myth of King Bladud and his pigs, it should be clear and obvious that the word 'Sulis' is a distinctive proper name, by the way in which it was spelt and by the manner in which it was used as a god-name in inscription. *If* this had been "suillus" (i.e. "Aquae suillus, the waters belonging to the pigs") it would surely have been spelt and referred to as such by the contemporary inscriptions. The distinction between SULIS referred to as a feminine power, and a word used in general language 'suillus' should be clear.

The physical attributes of the site itself suggest the goddess' name, and as has been suggested, the use of a native term is in keeping with the general practice of the Romans in Britain, where Celtic and Latin terms were continually put together, in god-names that refer directly to the environmental nature of the place, as well as to the divine powers worshipped there.

The meanings of "eye" "Gap" "Hole" "Whirlpool" further expand into related concepts of "far seeing" "sharp sighted" and "Knowing", and so confirm the possibility of the Celtic derivation of the name, for the goddess of the underworld was always the goddess of knowledge and prophecy. The relationship between "eye" and "whirlpool" is still used in modern language, where we talk about the "eye of a whirlpool" or the "eye of a storm". This is a reference to the still centre which supposed to exist according to the laws of nature, but was a concept well established in the ancient philosophy, and which features extensively in mystical terminology. Its origin is in the ancient Otherworld gate, over which the goddess presided.

It is interesting to note that in several myths, the Pig is an animal of the Otherworld, and was brought out of the depths for the benefit of mankind, by a hero, after an expedition or raid. The swine is therefore an animal-that-comes-up-from-the-gap; as it is natural that the mythical king Bladud is led to the gap where the waters originate by a herd of swine.

Recent finds from the central spring include an inscription that suggests that the name of the goddess was 'SUL' and not 'SULIS', but in either variant of the term, the root meaning suggested above may hold true. One of the problems of limited finds in inscription is that they do not always follow presumed grammatical rules, but 'SULIS' is thought to be the genitive of 'SUL'.

King Bladud Restored

Having collected all the little bits and pieces of Bladud, scattered from myth to monument, is it possible to fit them together in a manner that will make any sense? Is there the trace of a coherent story behind the evidence?

The answer is that there is *already* a group of stories which come so close to the pattern shown by the archaeology and legends associated with Aquae Sulis, that we may assume that a similar tale was woven into the religious use of the site.

The evidence discussed so far suggests that:

1. Bath originated as an oracular 'Otherworld' cult centre, under the power of a Celtic or pre-Celtic Mother Goddess.
2. The Goddess developed a myth-cycle common to such cults in the ancient world, supported by ritual and by therapeutic practices.
3. The entire structure was taken over by the Romans, who developed it considerably, and amalgamated the native cult with the strong classical elements which we can see today.
4. The carvings, the literary sources, and the structure of the site itself, suggest that there was a common myth, acceptable to both Romans and Celts.

The prime myth of this sort, known in many forms to Celts, Romans and Greeks, because of their common origins, was that of The-hero-who-conquers-a-Monster. This basic theme has already been discussed with regard to 'Medusa' and the male head from the Temple Pediment, but there are many other examples from classical and native sources.

The hero formed a bridge between mankind and the gods. He was more than a mere man (often of divine parentage on one side and human on the other), and his role was to act out certain power patterns of the gods and goddesses through his life. In the classical world, heroes were worshipped as lesser beings, second to the gods, although some of them were accepted as divine at the end of their tasks, while others failed to recognise their role, and were blasted for aspiring too high. The hero was constantly responsible for the *operation* of the evolutionary or repressive gifts of the gods and goddesses. The same sort of pattern applied to the Celtic heroes, who came into conflict with the older deities, or were aided by supernatural means.

A few typical examples of such stories are: *Bellerophon, or Hipponous*, who killed the Chimerea, a monster with three heads that breathed fire. He was given a winged horse, Pegasus, by Athena/Minerva. He later tried to ride this horse into the upper realms of the gods, but Zeus sent a gadfly to sting it, and Bellerophon was unseated, to become either lame or blind.

Heracles, on the eleventh of his twelve great labours, killed a hundred headed dragon, which guarded the golden apples of the Hesperides. The Hesperides were three sisters, described by the classical writer Hesiod (in his "Theogeny") as living on an island in the Western Ocean, and were called the Daughters of Night. When

Heracles killed the serpent or dragon, the sisters fled and he gave the golden apples to Athena/Minerva. She later put them back in the Garden.

Heracles was the epitome of the classical hero....while in his cradle he strangled two snakes....the beginning of a long career of monster killing. His twelve labours were set him as a penance or rebalancing process for the murder of his own children, which he had done while afflicted with madness by the goddess Hera, who had a grudge against him. He was advised to accept the tasks by the oracle of Appollo at Delphi, with which he had a relationship that varied from friendly to intensely hostile. The twelve labours, and his other heroic-magical acts, have often been interpreted as a solar myth, connected with the Seasons of the year and the Zodiac. Like the Celtic Arthur, he even descended into the Underworld as one of his marvellous achievements.

Similar stories are told about Perseus, Theseus, Jason and various other heroic characters. All of the above mentioned were aided by Athena/Minerva, except Theseus, whose arms and guidance were supplied by Ariadne, the Weaver Goddess.

The elements of the myth in classical form are that a goddess contrives a situation whereby a hero has to fight a malignant being. She helps him in various ways, and then receives the token of the battle, which she returns to its original place, or keeps for its original use. A close examination of these myths suggests that the monster is actually a negative aspect of the same goddess, and that the pattern is a cycle.

There are numerous parallels in Celtic stories:
Arthur and his men fight a giant boar, the Twrch Trwyth, a theme which occurs frequently in Celtic myth. The boar was a potent magical animal, of both malific and beneficial powers.
Diancecht, a god of healing, slew a giant serpent that was destroying cattle all over Ireland. (*Note again the connection between serpents, and gods of healing, such as Appollo*).
Finn MacCumhaill destroyed a vertible chain of serpents all over Ireland, each with various attributes of fire, water and death dealing powers.

Dragons and monstrous beasts and cattle feature in Welsh lore, and many of these Celtic monsters are actually transformed humans. In this guise they lead heroes into the Otherworld, or some magically demanding situation, and when conquered or questioned in the right manner, reveal their true identity. This is similar to the contrivance of the goddess Minerva or Athena, where the whole aim of the chase or conflict is to give benefit to the achieving hero. The courtly development of the Celtic transformation is to be found in the 'Loathsome Lady' stories, in which a knight is compelled by honour to wed a hideous hag. When she asks him if he would like her to be fair and lovely by day, or by night, he leaves the choice to her....and she becomes beautiful for ever. The addition to this story is of course the riddle 'What does woman want the most?', the answer to which, as the knight discovers, is 'Her own way'.

10.The position of The Head on the Roman style pediment of the Temple of Sulis Minerva. The pediment can be read as a statement of the pagan belief in the structure of the universe, very similar to the widespread "Tree of Life" symbolism known in most ancient religions, accounting for the stages between the Underworld below, the human and animal world, and the realms of the sun planets and

84

stars. Compare this photograph to the reconstruction offered by archaeologists, and the West Front of Bath Abbey, where the same concept has turned into the suppressive hierarchy of the Church and State. (Numbers 4 and 5).

85

If we grant that all these stories, in their numerous forms from basic hero battles to courtly philosophies, have the same pattern; how does the story of Bladud fit this pattern?

The story of Bladud has come to us in two parts, from two separate sources. The folk tale about the leprous pigs, from Pierces' memoirs, is the first part of the story, We then have another part, which is surely a *conclusion*, from the version given by Geoffrey or Tysilio, which is also derived from a native tradition.

Assuming the myth to follow the usual pattern, there should be a middle section, where Bladud battles with the monster, and wins, with the aid of the goddess to whom he later dedicated his Temple. The carving of the solar-head from the Temple Pediment shows a Victorious Sun, in Celtic guise....he has done battle, and won, with the aid of Minerva. There is an additional cultural implication in this carving, for a local myth has been Romanised. It would not be too daring to suggest that Bladud, as a hero, has conquered one of the fearsome monster-goddesses common to the Celts, aided by one of the culturally beneficial goddesses, later equated with Minerva. This comfortably mythologises the Roman conquest and adaptation of the site, while retaining the native element, probably with very little change. The secret, of course, was that the Goddess had her own way, for she was both the fearsome and the kindly aspects, and retained her power throughout, no matter what name she was known by.

An illness forces the hero into exile. He is led by totem beasts to a sacred site, which is guarded by a monster. He fights the guardian, aided by a helpful Goddess who symbolises common sense, wisdom and control, and he wins. His conquest makes him a hero-king, and he acquires magical powers, which he uses for the benefit of the people, and to the glory of the Goddess. Finally, he overreaches himself, and aspires to become a god. At this stage, he crashes into the Winter, and to his death.

The story is much more than a seasonal round, or even a cultural retrospective explanation. As has been suggested in the chapter on 'The Gorgon's Head' it can symbolise human evolution, and also an individual process of realisation which is well known in pyschotherapy.

In ritual magic of all periods of human development, or types of culture, a process evolves by which 'inner' dynamic situations are presented to the initiate. These situations were usually linked to wider cycles of life and death, and to the seasons, but had and still have a direct and personal validity also. The process was shown as a drama, or in the case of the cults where trance played an important part, as a controlled dream or vision based upon symbols which had been carefully studied in advance. The initiate or subject, or patient, has to act out the pattern, until he wins, or until the inner monster defeats him.

The public and secret rituals of the pagan cults often brought themes of this sort through into ritual drama, and such dramas can still be seen today in the various folk and 'mumming' plays which survive throughout Europe, with their basic death and resurrection theme, often involving the battle with a beast. The entire system of symbols was absorbed by Christianity and the Archangel Michael took over from the old sun-heroes, and suppressed the Serpent. By this time, the monster had become a symbol of evil, rather than one of uncontrolled passion or unbalanced energy, which is the role that it has in the pagan myths. The monsters or serpents, giant boars and bulls, all symbolise raw power, the life and death power of the Otherworld in an uncontrolled elemental form, expressed further by the image of the passionate and bloodthirsty goddess, such as the Morrigan. Beings such as St. Michael, and of course St. George, are very direct descendants of Hercules or Finn MacCumhaill, but with an added element of goodness, chivalry or honour, and an interpretation of morality that their pagan ancestors lacked. Indeed, the basic 'message' of the pagan myths is hardly 'moral' at all, as the hero is not rewarded for virtue, nor is he made good....only victorious and glorious. The conclusion that the ancient heroes offer us is that application to one kind of awareness or intelligence (symbolised by Minerva) is beneficial to humankind, while its opposite side has to be controlled or conquered. Too often the hero suffers from an excess of his success, and flies beyond his abilities, by which act he returns to unbalance and destruction. The story is cyclic, which is exactly what we should expect from a system rooted in observation of the natural world.

The Christian development, however, suggested a more permanent suppression of the primal forces, to be achieved by goodness or grace through the mediation of one specific Saviour. This was quite alien to the pagan concept of evolutionary self-help, heroic action, and the subtle round of death and life controlled by the Otherworld powers.

In their book 'Celtic Heritage' Alwyn and Brinley Rees include a very interesting note, which is directly relevant to the discussion of King Bladud, and his heroic role: "....we would pose a question of 'the fitness of names'; can the similarity, and interrelationship, of the names in the following paragraph be dismissed as 'mere' coincidence?

"The Irish Tuatha de *Danann* are obliged to come to terms first with the men of *Bolg*, finally with the descendants of *Bile* (father of Mil), and in their greatest battle their chief adversary is *Balor*, giant champion of the Sid. The father of Aranrhod, *Beli*, who appears as the progenitor of several Welsh dynasties, is perhaps the consort of *Don* while there is some evidence to suggest that the *Bellerus* whose story (according to Milton) was linked to the Cornish St. Michael's Mount, was, like the *Balor* of folk-tales, a one-eyed thieving giant. *Belenus* whose name occurs more frequently than any other Celtic god name in the inscriptions of the Roman period, is described as the patron of the *Danubian* province of Noricum; the giant or dragon of Roumanian folklore is *Balaur*. In Greek mythology, *Belus* is the father of *Danaus* and grandfather of the Danaids who kill their cousin-husbands, grandsons of *Belus*, and furthermore the Medusa is killed by the son of *Danae*, the Chimarea by *Bellerophon*. Lastly, the Indian *Bali*, mighty king of the Asuras, and sovereign of Patala, an underworld realm of riches, beauty and pleasure comparable with the (Celtic) Sid and Annwfn, conquers Indra and the gods — Indra who is born to be the slayer of the son of *Danu*. No two of these names, Beli, Bile, Bali, Bolg, Belus, Balor, Balaur, Bellerus, Bellerophon, Belenus — have been convincingly related to

87

one another philologically. But to disprove etymological relationship throughout would not necessarily be to dispose of our question". (*A. & B. Rees, Celtic Heritage, page 366*).

In some of the names listed above, the bright solar hero has become merged with the monster, a common process as one cult and culture succeeds to another, but the implication is clear. If Bladud is at all justifiable, via the pages of the old Chronicles, and the implication of the local folk tale, and the Temple Pediment, then he must at some time or other have slain a monster or dragon.

Perhaps the archaeological research planned for the near future will reveal some more carving or dedicatory material to shed fresh light on the story, but two theoretical candidates of beastliness immediately spring to mind from the evidence available. The prime importance of the pig, and the Celtic myth of the magical boar hunt (where a monster is actually leading the hero to benefit, which has to be won through effort) reinforced by the presence of pigs in the folk tale of Bladud, suggest that his monster could have been a giant boar. The classical tradition of the hero slaying giant serpents also has Celtic parallels, and there are images of Celtic heroes or gods holding up serpents, and wearing torques which are twin headed snakes. Snakes of this sort appear on the head carved at Bath, so he could have slain a serpent or dragon.

The Unfinished Story

Just as the myth of Bladud and similar figures has no final ending, and as Winter turns into Spring, so the story of Aquae Sulis itself has no obvious conclusion. The site still has an immense amount to offer, and its potential for excavation will probably never be fully realised.

The basic elements in archaeology, symbology, and literature have been analysed, but there are always additions to these elements, some in the most surprising places. A carving of Appollo, with his lyre, is built into the Church at Compton Dando, nine miles from Bath. This is thought to be part of the sacrificial altar from the Temple of Sulis Minerva, and its appearance in the buttress of a Christian worship place is probably due to the fact that the Bath Convent once owned Compton Dando church. Pagan remains were often built into Christian structures, for magical or superstitious reasons, but it is intriguing to speculate as to how and when the medieval monastic builders found Appollo and the other figure carved with him, as no record of the transfer or discovery is known.

Future excavations in Bath may reveal more statutory, and will undoubtedly extend practical knowledge of the buildings during the Roman period. The origin of Aquae Sulis, and its growth from primitive environmental worship into an important centre, is a solid proof of the evolution of human belief; and it offers us that proof in a coherent and often beautiful sequence. We are fortunate indeed to have such a clearly defined site, with its added traditional and literary elements.

Bath is not only important in the recovery of Roman British cultural history, but also as evidence of the pattern of pagan worship. It reinforces theoretical and literary evidence of ancient beliefs with good solid stone, and suggests that the level of civilisation during the early period of Roman development may have been higher than is often thought. There is also a significant pan-cultural element to Aquae Sulis, which conclusively states that the Romans did *not* encounter savages when they took over the use of the hot springs, but that they merged with people who had a developed culture of their own. There was a common ground between the native Celts, the incoming Romanised Celts from the mainland, and the other Imperial subjects under military and civil direction. This common ground was a body of belief, epitomised in central myths, and derived from environmental worship in primitive times.

Only the Roman talent for construction, amalgamation, and order could have elevated Aquae Sulis to its peak of growth and expression; only the tenacity and vigour of the Celtic traditions could have preserved the mythical and magical content visibly within that civilised framework.

Photographs

by Simon Ferguson   1978

1. The outlet from the Roman reservoir. The cave-like effect of the arch above the monolithic capstone may well have acquired magical or symbolic value to the Celts and Romans as the cleft that led into the Otherworld....the entry to the hot springs. It was used as an outlet from the reservoir, though this use varied and may not have been constant. The enclosed area retains a powerful and impressive atmosphere to this day, an intuitive insight into the worship of the pagans.

2. A very primitive representation of the "Three Mothers" or Triple Goddess, shown in the museum at Bath, although not directly from the site of the springs.

3. The goddess Luna. Shown in head and shoulders relief, she is supported by a device which shows both full and crescent moons, and horns, as one symbolic disc. Her hair is tied up to represent sea-shells, showing her rule over the tides, and she carries a staff and thong, or whip, as an emblem of power and control. This implement may represent her rule over horses, which would integrate this image with the widespread Celtic goddess of horses, who was one of the major native deities. Cunliffe suggests that this image would have fitted over the facade of the Four Seasons, which he proposes for reasons of architectural harmony. Curiously, the Celts reckoned their seasons by lunar and not solar calculations, so the structural possibility of such a placement of the Luna pediment may have some symbolic background that bridges classical and native use, as is very plain with the solar pediment that fronted the Temple of Sulis Minerva.

4. The stylised head of the Celtic Sun God, Belinus or Bel, identified by the Greeks and Romans with Appollo. His waving flaming hair discloses his wings and ears, typical solar attributes for an all-seeing all-hearing god. Although the head is constructed in such a way as to be a full face in flattened relief, similar to metalwork of the period, the presence of two intertwined snakes around the lower part may suggest a torque, the Celtic neck ornament of magical power, which symbolised the union with the forces of nature. This head is likely to be that of the being referred to by Geoffrey of Monmouth as "King Bladud", a master of magic and necromancy in the Druid tradition.

5. A native carving of the goddess Minerva. A faint head can be seen upon her breast, which radiates lines. Is this the Gorgon's head that turned all who gazed upon it to stone?

6. The West Front of Bath Abbey. Here the "earth to heaven" concept first seen in the pagan Temple Pediment, is repeated, but with a Christian and authoritarian emphasis.

7. A restoration of the Temple Pediment, built in Sydney Gardens, Bath. The design is hopelessly out of keeping with the classical principles made clear in the reconstruction given by Cunliffe and Richmond and Toynbee, and has distinctly been influenced by the "Gorgon" theory, to such an extent that the head carved here is full of writhing snakes, which are not present upon the original.

8. Ritual mask, from the Temple area. This mask bears a close resemblance to similar items found in Europe, and is very near in style to the traditional ritual mask used in the Padstow May ceremony. The Padstow ceremony, a folk custom of undoubted pagan

91

origin, includes a death-and resurrection sequence, the character St. George (who is a rationalisation of a sun-god), and until only a few years ago, involved reverence of a spring and water source. Such traditional ceremonies often provide an insight into early religious practices, particularly when they are compared to classical references.

9. The statue of King Bladud over the "Kings Bath", above the source of the main hot Spring. This statue was said to have replaced an older city effigy, a custom common to many cities, which dates back to pagan belief in the power of guardian images connected with distinct localities.

10.The position of The Head on the Roman style pediment of the Temple of Sulis Minerva. The pediment can be read as a statement of the pagan belief in the structure of the universe, very similar to the widespread "Tree of Life" symbolism known in most ancient religions, accounting for the stages between the Underworld below, the human and animal world, and the realms of the sun planets and stars. Compare this photograph to the reconstruction offered by archaeologists, and the West Front of Bath Abbey, where the same concept has turned into the suppressive hierarchy of the Church and State. (Numbers 4 and 5).

A Short Bibliography

The following list suggests titles for further reading. Many of these works contain bibliographies. In addition to classical and authoritative modern sources, several unusual and speculative titles have been included, and these are marked with an asterisk (*).

CEASAR, Julius. (tr. 1963) S.A. Handford. "The Conquest of Gaul". London.
CUNLIFFE, B. (1969). "Roman Bath". Society of Antiquaries. (Plus other authoritative works on Bath, Rome, the Celts and allied subjects).
DONOVAN, J. (1868). ed. W. Stokes. Translation of "Cormac's Glossary". Calcutta.
DUDLEY, D.R. & Webster. (1962). "The Rebellion of Boudicca". London.
EVANS, J.G. (1906). Translation of "The Black Book of Carmarthen". Pwllheli.
EVANS, J.G. (1910). Translation of "The Book of Taliesin". Lanbedrog.
FERGUSON, J. (1970). "The Religions of the Roman Empire". London.
FRAZER, J.G. (1960). "The Golden Bough" abridged. London.
GANTZ, G. (1976). Translation "The Mabinogion". London.
GRANT, M. (1978). "History of Rome". London.
GRAVES, R.* (1975). "The White Goddess". London.
HERODOTUS. (1954). Translation A. de Selincourt. "The Histories". London.
HERM, G. (1976). "The Celts". London.
HOLE, C. (1975). "English Traditional Customs". London.
JENNINGS, H.* (1887). "The Rosicrucians". London.
JOURNAL OF ROMAN STUDIES. Various.
KNIGHT, G. (1978). "A history of White Magic". Oxford.
LEVIS, H.C. (1919 & 1973). "The British King Who Tried to Fly". Bath.
MacCANA, P. (1970). "Celtic Mythology". London.
MacCULLOCH, J.A. (1911). "The Religion of the Ancient Celts" Edinburgh.
MEYER, K. (1906). Translation. "The Death Tales of the Ulster Heroes". Dublin.
MONMOUTH, Geoffrey. (Tr. 1963). "History of the Kings of Britain". Sebastian Evans. London.
PIGGOT, S. (1965). "The Druids". London.
REES. A & B. (1961). "Celtic Heritage". London.
ROSS. A. (1974). "Pagan Celtic Britain". London.
ROSS. A. Other works on related subjects.
RUTHERFORD, W. (1978). "The Druids and their Heritage". London.
SICULUS, Diodorus. (Tr. 1933). "The History..." C.H. Oldfather. London.
SPENCE, L.* "The History of Atlantis". London.
STEWART, B. (1977). "Where is St. George?". Bradford on Avon.
STEWART, B. (1980). "The Myth of King Bladud". Bath.
STRABO. Translation. "The Geography". H.C. Jones. London.
TACITUS. (Tr. 1964). "The Histories". K. Wellesley. London.
TACITUS. (Tr. 1948). "On Britain & Germany". H. Mattingly. London.
WIMBERLEY, L.C. (1959). "Folklore in the English and Scottish Ballads". New York.

THE AUTHOR

Bob Stewart is an author, composer, and musician. In addition to 'Waters of The Gap' he has published works and articles on mythology, folklore and musical instruments. He has recorded five long-playing records of his own songs and compositions, and of arrangements of traditional folk music. He has also written music and songs for theatre, television, feature films, and radio. As a performer and lecturer, he has toured extensively in Europe, the United States of America, and in Great Britain.

Also by Bob Stewart...

"The Myth of King Bladud" *Bath City 1980*
"Where is St. George?" *Moonraker Press 1977*
"The Giant who ate Porridge" *MacMillan (for children)*

Discs

"The Unique Sound of the Psaltery" *Argo zda 207*
"The Wraggle Taggle Gypsies O" *Cresent Ars 105*
"Up Like the Swallow" *Broadside BRO 131*
"Tomorrow We Part" *Broadside BRO 133*

94